*Discover the Proof, the Power
and the Magic of Manifesting
Genuine Abundance*

THE
LAWYER

&

THE
LAW OF
Attraction

Paula Kidd Casey J.D.

BALBOA
PRESS
A DIVISION OF HAY HOUSE

Scripture quotations marked KJV are from the Holy Bible, King James Version (Authorized Version). First published in 1611. Quoted from the KJV Classic Reference Bible, Copyright © 1983 by The Zondervan Corporation.

Balboa Press books may be ordered through booksellers or by contacting:

Balboa Press
A Division of Hay House
1663 Liberty Drive
Bloomington, IN 47403
www.balboapress.com
1 (877) 407-4847

Print information available on the last page.

ISBN: 978-1-5043-9402-4 (sc)
ISBN: 978-1-5043-9404-8 (hc)
ISBN: 978-1-5043-9403-1 (e)

Library of Congress Control Number: 2017919301

Balboa Press rev. date: 02/22/2018

"Your work is to discover your world
and then with all your heart,
give yourself to it."
Buddha

"Believe nothing unless it agrees with your common sense."
Buddha

"We now have the scientific tools that allow us to use our
logic and common sense to embrace the
mystical aspect of our soul."
Paula Kidd Casey

To My Universe:
My husband, my children and my grandchildren

My opening argument

May it please the doubters of the Universe:

I stand before you as an attorney—a logical, rational professional who will provide proof of a Magical Universe.

I have compiled evidence that will withstand scrutiny, and I present it herein.

You will hear the personal testimonies of individuals who, using the Natural Laws of the Universe, manifested their dreams.

I will present testimony from qualified experts who, after careful research, discovered the workings of the Natural Laws.

I will offer peer-reviewed scientific data that solidifies the teachings of the Ancient Masters of Truth.

I will then submit actions one may take to access the Magic of the Cosmos.

All I ask of you realists is to keep an open mind and an open heart.

Although tangible evidence can convince your intellect, it is your heart that has the final vote.

In a court of law, the burden of proof is beyond a reasonable doubt.

In the court of doubters, the burden of proof is beyond your current beliefs.

I can only provide evidence to satisfy your brain. You must provide the faith of a mustard seed to risk a new belief and satisfy your soul.

I ask you to find that the Universe is Magical, Conscious, and always looking out for you.

I will never rest my case.

Respectfully submitted,
Paula Kidd Casey, Esq.

Contents

Introduction

I always wanted to believe in magic. I would watch *Peter Pan* and jump off the couch, absolutely certain I could fly. I would try to stay awake to catch a glimpse of the tooth fairy. I would wish on a star and fall asleep dreaming it would come true.

Somewhere along the line, I replaced the word *magic* with *money*. Money would bring me the outcome I desired. I packed away the magic with my baby doll and turned my attention to reality and making money.

I have made lots of money, and the stress it took to make it almost killed me. I also have been one paycheck away from penniless, and the stress of not having enough money was debilitating.

This became a vicious cycle: stressful productivity, accumulation of money, mindless spending on inconsequential dribble, and a balance sheet written in red ink.

I saw no way off this hamster wheel. Until … until I discovered the magic that was there all along. I found a way to reconnect to my Authentic Self, to remember my Divine Inheritance and to truly understand what abundance meant, more specifically, what abundance meant to me.

Have you been there? Wanting something more? Not even being able to define what it would look like? Buying, reading, and screaming at all the self-help books you could get your hands on to no avail? Wanting the Law of Attraction, or the Seven Habits, or The Seven Spiritual Laws to work for you but not immediately seeing your wish list materialize, tossing the books into the trash (hopefully the recycle bin)?

The big question is: Why didn't it work for me?

It took me years of searching, reading, and listening to the greatest teachers in the world to find the answer, to find the magic. And not meaning to sound pretentious, I have.

Gen-u-ine: truly what something is said to be; authentic, sincere, real, actual; not counterfeit.

A-bun-dance: a large quantity of something; the state or condition of having a copious quantity of something; plenty, bounty, wealth.

I thought I had achieved *genuine abundance* and had played the game of success well. Coming from a loving, middle-class family in a small Midwestern town, I put myself through college and then law school. I opened my own law firm two years after law school and ran it successfully for over thirty-seven years. I married, had a precious baby, and divorced, while still practicing law successfully. I was a single mom for a while, juggling work, parenthood, stress, and life. I remarried, made more money, and bought a bigger home. I adopted another precious child, worked harder, made more money, and bought an even bigger house.

We lived in a five-bedroom home in a prestigious area of Wichita, Kansas. My children went to the best private school. We bought a second home in Breckenridge, Colorado. My daughter went to an expensive out-of-state college and had a gorgeous wedding after graduation. I thought I had it all: a wonderful, loving family; two beautiful homes; and a successful career.

Until one Sunday afternoon in late January 2006. I was in my home office while the Super Bowl, which I had agreed to watch with my husband, played in the family room. Not being a big football fan and annoyed at my husband, I wasn't motivated to be with either. I was fiddling and fidgeting in the office when pain erupted from my chest. I felt light-headed and couldn't catch my breath. I screamed at my husband that I was having a heart attack. He yelled back, "Can you wait until halftime?" Whaaat? Fast-forward six months. After a trip to the hospital (not waiting until halftime) and six-month's worth of tests, the doctor gave me the news. There was nothing wrong with me; it was all in my head. The news did not sit well with me. I am strong and stubborn and professional and persistent and in total control of my life (and everyone else's life in the general vicinity). I am not crazy or lazy or weak or, well, crazy. I refused to accept the fact that there was not a thing wrong with me physically or accept the fact that what was wrong with me was emotional.

But no amount of complaining, denying it was all emotional, or demanding that there was something physically wrong with me changed the doctors' prognosis. I was depressed and having anxiety attacks, they said. Well, I was depressed because there was something horribly wrong with me that those quacks couldn't discover, and I didn't have anxiety attacks! They are reserved for the weak, meek nonproducers, not movers and shakers like me. The more I got upset, the more attacks I would have.

Hmmm, a connection?

The prescribed medication didn't work, and the "attacks" continued. For those mover and shakers and strong people out there who have never had an anxiety attack, let me tell you about them. You think you are dying. You feel you must get away from the pain and the horrible sensation and try to run away from ... yourself. It doesn't work. You want to sit down, lie down, get up, run away, or stand still. What I ended up doing most of the time was sitting in the corner in a fetal position, rocking and telling myself it had to end sometime, either in the conclusion of the attack—or death.

I knew I couldn't go on like this, and I needed to do something. Because I was an attorney and knew how to research data, I hired myself to find a solution. Assuming I was having anxiety attacks, what could I do to regain control of my life and, of course, the world? I ordered a program that was marketed to work for anxiety. It contained ten CDs to listen to daily. I found myself arguing with the poor presenter. I would cross-examine her: What are your credentials? Have you been qualified as an expert witness? What verified data do you have that supports your position? I would object for lack of foundation and request that a line be stricken from the record (remembering of course this was a CD). I was a mess.

The information being presented was based on cognitive behavioral conditioning, a well-respected area of psychology. It didn't help very much. But it did remind me of some books I had read in the '90s, books I had liked and that had somehow touched my soul. They were, however, very "woo-woo" (a legal term meaning new age ideas, New Thought philosophy, and, well, woo-woo). I dug them out and read them. Hmmm, some relief.

I looked at more books that resonated with me: *The Power of Now* by Eckhart Tolle, books on the Buddha, books by Deepak Chopra, books in the alternative section of Barnes & Noble. More relief. So for the next five years I read hundreds of books on how your thoughts control your life, on how we had the power all along, my dear (okay, so I watched *The Wizard of Oz*). I started meditating and breathing and just sitting in silence. Getting better.

I loved this genre and read everything I could get my hands on. I concluded there was a Barnes & Noble angel because every time I went there I found the perfect book. One day I was walking through the science aisle on the way to the alternative section when a book literally fell off the shelf in front of me. It was *The God Theory* by astrophysicist Dr. Bernard Haisch, a book bridging science with spirituality. I was hooked. I had to find the verified data and documented experiments that proved this "thought becomes things" stuff was based in science as well as the ethereal. I continued my research.

I found quantum physics. Although it is defined as "the study of subatomic particles and electromagnetic waves that act in very strange ways," what it is, is just darn magical! Without getting into specifics, which are difficult to understand and discussed at more length in the science chapter, new scientific discoveries have validated ancient teachings—that our consciousness (our soul, our living-ness) actually creates our environment.

I decided I would take my years of training in legal research and find documentation uniting the spiritual information shared by the masters with valid scientific data, uniting quantum physics and the natural laws of vibration and attraction.

I had found my passion. I wanted to learn and then teach this information. What was to become the first of many coincidences that now appear constantly in my life, I stumbled upon "Notes from the Universe," a daily email from Mike Dooley, an amazing mentor who gave me sage advice from the cosmos. Loving the notes, I again did research and found that Mike Dooley, the self-proclaimed Universe who penned the notes, was offering a training session to teach these concepts to others in a workshop forum. I signed up, traveled to Orlando, and became a certified trainer for "Infinite Possibilities," a program based on the book of the same name. I taught workshops in my dining room to other seekers and served on a panel of trainers at the National Conference of Infinite Possibilities six months later. A year after I found this treasure, I was fortunate enough to be asked to be a presenter at the National Conference of Infinite Possibilities in January 2013.

Wanting to take this information even deeper and reach more people, especially professionals and entrepreneurs, I once again stumbled onto the perfect platform for me, authored by another beloved mentor, Bob Proctor. The program, "Thinking into Results," was geared toward business and based on science. I became a certified consultant for this program in September 2014.

I have been teaching these principles for the past three years, reaching more people. But once again I knew I needed to expand to reach even more.

"What you are seeking is seeking you."

I am seeking those people who, although they may not have had heart attacks, know that their heart is attacking them, whispering to them, "It's time to explore, to grow, to learn, to find genuine abundance."

For you see, although I thought I had it all that Sunday in January 2006, I found that what I *had* was not what my spirit wanted but what had been programmed into me since birth. My spirit, my heart, knew my path was different from the one I had been on and needed to "attack" me to get my attention. The attacks in which I felt I must get away from "me" were a stern suggestion to get away from "that self" and find my "true self."

So, for the past ten years I have been on this journey of discovery, peeling away layers of conditioning and finding the magic and my joy. My genuine abundance. If I can shorten your journey by sharing mine, I will be honored. If I can share with you the information on how our conditioning controls what we become or do, and how we can choose a new path and reprogram that conditioning so we can access this magical universe, I will celebrate. If I can help you find your genuine abundance, I will feel fulfilled. I am seeking you.

Let's first look at the conditioning most people are exposed to from birth and how this programming prevents us from using the Natural Laws to our advantage and achieving our desired results.

Second, we will delve into the amazing, magical Natural Laws and how to use them to our benefit. When we better understand these concepts, a portal appears into the world of genuine abundance, of wealth, of passion, of relationships, and of possibilities.

Finally, I offer the scientific foundation that unites these laws with science (for those of you who require verified data), thus allowing you to be able to logically embrace the magic of genuine abundance.

Chapter 1

- -

Abundance, or the Lack Thereof

Joe Somebody was born into a nice middle-class family who loved him very much. Because they loved him so much, they wanted to keep him safe. And because they wanted to keep him safe, they did what all parents do who love their children—taught him about life by teaching him the rules their parents taught them:

- Don't do that—you'll put your eye out.
- Clean your plate—children are starving in China.
- Put that back—we can't afford it.
- Put that up—you can't shave the cat.
- Don't buy that—money doesn't grow on trees.
- Don't jump off the roof—you'll break your neck.
- Pick something else—we're not made of money.
- You can't have that—there's only so much to go around.

All sound advice and based on Joe's parent's knowledge of life. Joe went to school and learned even more:

- He learned to regurgitate information.
- He learned to quit daydreaming.
- He learned to think the way the old textbooks told him to think.

- He learned to pick a trade to fall back on because dreams don't pay the bills.
- He learned you must work hard to make money.

Quite simply, he learned to settle.

Joe went to college to learn a trade because dreams don't pay bills. He got married, bought a small house, and had two wonderful children. He loved his children very much so he taught them about life.

He scrimped and saved because money doesn't grow on trees. He wanted to buy his family nice things and travel with his kids, but he couldn't afford that.

Joe still dreamed his childhood dreams, but he never pursued them because they don't pay the bills and he wasn't made of money. Joe settled.

Joe spent much of his time worrying about money and the lack of it. His lack of money consumed much of his time as he tried to make his money match his month. He knew he had to work hard to make money, so he worked harder.

Joe loved his family very much and was thankful for what he had. He felt guilty for wanting more because there was only so much to go around. He never jumped off a roof or broke his neck. He didn't put an eye out and never shaved a cat. Joe couldn't afford the things he wanted because he knew money was tight and didn't grow on trees, and he put things back because he hadn't worked harder to get more money. Joe learned his lessons well.

Years marched by. Joe got old and sick. As he lay on his deathbed reflecting on his life of hard work, of scrimping and saving to get by, and of unfulfilled dreams, a stranger burst in.

The stranger held up an envelope and breathlessly panted, "Joe, I've been meaning to tell you about this. You have a savings account with millions of dollars in it. It's yours for the taking. You can do anything you want. It's always been available for you to access. Sorry you didn't know about it sooner. Here you go."

Joe sat up and in his dying breath said, "Well, that sucks. What I wouldn't have given to have known about it sooner."

I'm here to inform you that you do have an account containing untold riches that is accessible at any time. I will show you exactly how to get it, the name and location of the institution, and the account number, and then hand you the keys.

If this is true, would you buy and read this book and do exactly what it says? Well, fish out that credit card and head for the checkout because the information contained herein can do just that. (Realizing, of course, Joe's story is a metaphor and the institution that contains your abundance is not a brick-and-mortar building—but just as accessible.)

The information in this book comes from many sources:

1. Natural Laws of the Universe
2. Masters of all cultures and time periods
3. Contemporary teachers and books
4. Especially science (for those left-brained, logical cynics)!

It's a compilation of many ideas and truths that are proven, as reliable as gravity, and oh so much fun to learn. And when put into practice, the rewards are abundant.

The information shared herein is the path to the *awareness* of who you really are and what you really can do, be, and have.

The only thing that keeps you from your dreams (big, exciting, and scary) is not having the *awareness* of how to achieve them.

Awareness seems to be the operative word here. How do we get this awareness? Let's be adventurous and find the answer on the Awareness Trail.

So saddle up because we are on a journey of discovery—and you will never be the same again.

Abundance Is Not a Four-Letter Word

"I have come that they may have life, and that they may have it more abundantly." —John 10:10

We need to get the ground rules straight. We are leaving our preconceived notions of lack and unworthiness at the door. We all have them: I'm not good enough, pretty enough, smart enough, rich enough to _____ (fill in the blank). Kick them off like we do our shoes at a snotty friend's front door. Come on this trek with an open mind and an open heart.

First and foremost, *abundance* is not a four-letter word. It is not something to be hidden, apologized for, or whispered about. God does not want you to be poor, contrary to what many organized institutions may lead you to believe. We were born to have abundance.

"The Lord will open to you His good treasure, the heavens, to give the rain to your land in its season, and to bless all the work of your hand." —Deuteronomy 28:12

We are so afraid to look abundance in the eye.

"Well, I'll take a little," you say. "Can't be selfish. Just enough to get by."

You weren't made in the image of God just to get by. Did God (Source, the Universe) make enough just to get by? Did He stop at creating just one star and say, "Okay, I guess I have enough light to read a book and stay warm"?

No! He wanted to see amazing galaxies and pet amazing animals and converse with amazing angels. He didn't stop at mediocre. He demanded abundance in all things, and so should you.

And for you to be able to appreciate all of what this amazing universe offers, you must have a "currency" that allows you to afford these opportunities. You must trade some of your "energy" (that for which you have traded your time or your creations) to other people who in turn trade their energy to you: exciting travel, sumptuous food, and comfortable shelter.

It is not selfish or evil to want to experience this wonderful world, to play all the wonderful games, and to create a wonderful life. Until you realize that it is your birthright to love and participate in all aspects of this planet you call home, you will never claim all the abundance that will allow you a full life.

Claiming abundance does not mean taking away something from someone else. It doesn't mean competing for a limited supply, with some having more and leaving some with less.

When you understand abundance, you understand there is an unlimited supply of energy, and you discover how to create it.

Genuine abundance means defining what an abundant life means to you and spending your currency on the things you value, so you don't end up spending this energy on inconsequential dribble.

Wallis Wattles, author of *The Science of Getting Rich*, eloquently explained this dictate from the Universe:

"The right to be rich ... the fact remains that is not possible to live a complete and successful life unless one is rich. No one can rise to his greatest possible height of talent or soul development unless he has plenty of money. To develop the soul and the talent he must have many things to use, and he cannot have these things unless he has the money to buy them with ... Therefore, the basis of all advancement must be the science of getting rich ... the object of all things is development, and everything that lives has an inalienable right to all the development it is capable of attaining. A person's right to life means he has the right to use all the things that may be necessary to his fullest unfolding. Success in life is becoming what you want to be, and you can only have the use of things when you can become rich enough to buy them ... If you neglect this study, you are derelict in your duty to yourself, to God, and to humanity, for you can render to God and to humanity no greater service than to make the most of yourself."

We have a duty to use our talents to create the most abundant life we can. Steve Bow once said, "God's gift to you is more talent and ability that you could possibly use in your lifetime. Your gift to God is to develop as much of that talent and ability as you can in this lifetime." Jesus told the parable of the talents. (Here *talents* means money, but how cool they called it talents, as we all have talents we can develop.) To paraphrase drastically, the servant who tripled his given talents was richly rewarded, and the servant who buried his talents, doing nothing with them, was stripped of even that.

"For whoever has, to him more will be given, and he will have abundance; but whoever does not have, even what he has will be taken away from him." —Matthew 13:12

The Universe, God, Source, or Infinite intelligence wants us to grow our lives, our talents, and our bank accounts. Divinity wants us to have abundance. If we squander our opportunities and don't develop our God-given talents, our lives naturally contract instead of expand. Expansion is the natural direction of the Universe and it should be ours as well.

Abundance is real and achievable and, well, abundant. It does not just mean monetary wealth, but abundance will always include as much monetary wealth as needed to obtain all the things that make your life rich in body, mind, and soul. It is yours for the asking. There is no lack or scarcity.

Okay, stop your argument right here. I know you will tell me about the starving children in China. We all remember the reason we cleaned our plates when we were little. (I am still a little hazy on why eating everything on our plates somehow helped those children. I actually think we were rubbing it in, but I digress.) Everything the masters teach works for all people equally. The natural laws we will discuss work as equally well for the Chinese children as it does for you, but I doubt they are reading this book at the moment. I do not mean to be uncaring, but pity and handouts have not eradicated the wretchedness of poverty in all of human history.

The best thing you can do for them is to learn this information, implement it, get abundantly wealthy, and go teach and help them.

Let me prove how abundance is rampant in your life.

There is an abundance of air, of water, of smiles, of love, and of gratitude.

There is an abundance of health. There is not a rationing of health, in which only so many people can be healthy at a time.

There is an abundance of knowledge and information. Did you know that 76 percent of people in the world have the Internet and access to 100 percent of all the information ever cataloged? There is an abundance of ideas, dreams, and thoughts. And when you realize where abundance truly comes from, you will realize how unlimited it is.

"Hey, but I want, like, an abundance of money," you say.

"You can have as much money as you believe you can," I tell you.

"But there is only so much money to go around," you say. "Those rich, greedy bastards have the largest part of the pie."

"Make another pie," I reply. "There is an abundance of ingredients for an infinite number of pies. You just have to know where to look." (Think this is a conundrum? Make a commitment to yourself to finish this book and find the answer.)

There is an abundance of imagination and willpower. You can choose a variety of perceptions and directions in your life. Your dream may not be to become filthy (what an adjective) rich, but I can almost bet you must have some cash to attain it. Making your life rich does not necessarily mean making your bank account explode, but it does mean knowing what stirs your soul and having the ability to obtain it.

"That's really what wealth does for you. It gives you freedom to make choices." —Oprah Winfrey

"There's a wealth that has nothing to do with dollars, that comes from the perspective and wisdom of paying attention to your life." —Oprah Winfrey

"I had no idea that being your authentic self could make me as rich as I've become. If I had, I'd have done it a lot earlier."
—Oprah Winfrey

"The journey to financial freedom starts the *minute* you decide you were destined for prosperity, not scarcity—for abundance, not lack. Isn't there a part of you that has always known that? Can you see yourself living a bounteous life—a life of more than enough? It only takes one minute to decide. Decide now."
—Mark Victor Hansen

"The cause of poverty is not scarcity. It is fear and small thinking." —Alan Cohen

"There is no lack in the world. The lack is in you, and if you will stop seeking lack and stop thinking lack … you will make marvelous demonstrations." —Al Koran

Abundance means you have all that is needed to live the life of your dreams. Think of that for a moment. Feel the feelings you would have if this might be true: the satisfaction, the relief, the contentment, the opportunities, the freedom to do what you love, the wisdom to recognize your truly amazing gifts, the authenticity to appreciate them.

You have a responsibility, a divine commandment, to accomplish what your heart desires. To do less is to squander your birthright, to insult the Universe.

Exercises

1. What would abundance look like in your life? Be as specific as possible in as many areas of your life as you can. List where you wish to live, what your dream home looks like, who you share it with, where you travel, what your vehicle looks like, what charities you give to, what your leisure time looks like, and how you grow your life.

2. What would it feel like if you had this abundance? Literally feel the emotions you would experience if you possessed this abundance. Take each category and list as many emotions for that specific goal as you can imagine: love, contentment, pride, respect, fulfillment, excitement, anticipation, eagerness, gratitude, satisfaction, accomplishment, happiness. Keep going; these are just to get you started!

Chapter 2

Dream Weaver

Everyone's abundance destination may be different, but the journey is always the same. Every stage of the journey is important, especially the very first step. As Confucius said, "A journey of a thousand miles begins with a single step."

Before you take that first step, however, it is essential that you each set the final destination, the desired result you wish to achieve. Just as you wouldn't leave for a long-anticipated vacation without any idea of where you are going, you shouldn't live your life without a plan for achieving what you desire.

You need to be very clear on that desired goal but very flexible on the route used to get there. The *goal* is the final destination, the ultimate vision of where you wish to see yourselves. The *journey* is the process, the ability to put into practice the concepts we will master in this book. The *route* is the direction; it is the way the Universe guides your steps to this ultimate outcome. Let the Universe decide on the route, stay flexible, take the first step, and set your goal.

It's time to set a desired outcome.

Most people when pressed to do so, will say (1) "I don't know what I want," or (2) "I am happy where I am." The first part of that sentence is an excuse and, in fact, a cop-out; the second part is a lack of awareness.

Let's deal with the first part of this sentence, "I don't know what I want." The *excuse* is based on the fact that we have forgotten how to dream of that amazing life we have always wanted. We don't know what steps we need to take to achieve it. We think it's not possible, so we abandon it. Whether by lack of early positive encouragement or just getting tired of being disappointed, we settle and rationalize that is how the world works.

Pretend with me for a moment that this is not how the world works. Pretend the world works in two different ways, depending on how we choose to look at it.

Assume there are two different envelopes offered to us in this lifetime, and we can choose which envelope we want.

"Everyone comes to this earth blessed with the privilege of controlling his mind power and directing it in any way he may choose," said Andrew Carnegie, the early twentieth-century magnate. "But everyone brings over with him at birth the equivalent of two sealed envelopes."

Let's look at our two choices.

Carnegie continues, "One is clearly labeled the riches you may enjoy if you take possession of your own mind and direct it toward the ends of your own choice. The other is labeled the penalties you must pay if you neglect to take possession of your own mind and direct it."

Carnegie further said, "In the one labeled 'Riches' is this list of blessings: sound health, peace of mind, a labor of love of your own choice, freedom from fear and worry, a positive mental attitude, and material riches of your own choice and quantity."

In the envelope labeled "Penalties" is this "list of prices you must pay for neglecting to take possession of your own mind: ill health, fear and worry, indecision and doubt, frustration and discouragement throughout life, poverty and want, and a whole flock of evils consisting of envy, greed, jealousy, anger, hatred, and superstition."

We must decide at this very moment to choose to take control of our mind and learn how to direct it toward the accomplishment of our dreams. Take off the blinders, the cloak of discouragement, and the sense of resignation, and decide to control your mind and begin to use your imagination.

Ask yourself, "What is the biggest dream I've ever had?" Perhaps it's something you thought was totally out of reach:

- To own a dream home?
- To be free to travel?
- To have money to buy a loved one's gifts?
- To start a movement, make a difference?
- To start a new career?
- To retire with abundance?

It's never too late, or too early for that matter, to look to the future with reckless abandon. Yes, I said reckless.

We must abandon old ways of thinking and planning, and begin to think and plan in a completely new way. We have historically chosen the wrong envelope and neglected to take control of our minds. Let's choose the "Riches" envelope instead.

"We must be willing to get rid of the life we've planned so as to have the life that is waiting for us," said Joseph Campbell.

How do we begin? It all starts with making a decision to take that first step. And our first step is to get clear on what our desire is. So go get a piece of paper. (It's not too hard yet.) Now draw a line right down the middle. At the top of the left-hand side, write the title "What I Don't Want." On the right side of the paper, write "What I Want." We are going to use a natural law of the universe here, the Law of Polarity: Everything has an opposite: left-right, up-down, front-back, here-there, now-then, etc. It's a time-space thing.

Now list as many things on the left side as you can think of. Get more paper if needed, but write, write like the wind. Get it all out. I'll wait. Done? Good.

Now, on the right side of the page, write the exact opposite of what is on the left side. Don't judge or compromise; just write the exact opposite. Example:

Don't want to work eight to five	Want flexibility
Hate working for someone	Work for myself
Hate feeling trapped	Want more freedom

When you are finished, look at the right side of the sheet and start circling words that are repetitious or that touch something deep inside you. On a blank piece of paper, list the ones you have circled in random order. Let your mind wander with imagination while you are reading and thinking about them.

Then ask yourself these questions about the circled concepts as if you already have those happy, positive conditions in your life.

- How do you spend your days? (I'm voting for sleeping, reading, writing, traveling, creating, being with loved ones, or building something.)
- What does your home look like (a McMansion, a tiny house, a backpack)?
- Who do you share your life with?
- What does your body and health look like?
- How much money do you have in savings and investments?
- How does it feel to be debt free?

Write your answers in cursive. Writing in cursive engages a creative part of the brain that allows you to explore new ideas and concepts. Quiet your mind and see what your hand creates on the page while you are thinking of the questions.

"Cursive handwriting stimulates brain synapses and synchronicity between the left and right hemispheres, something absent from printing and typing," wrote Suzanne Baruch Anderson in "The Benefits of Cursive Go Beyond Writing" (*New*

York Times, April 30, 2013). "Cursive therefore is vital in mastering the standards of written expression and critical thinking."

And John Hagelin, a renowned quantum physicist, notes, "In handwriting, while the hand appears to write, in reality it is the mind that writes."

Bob Proctor, one of my mentors, proposes that there are only three lifestyle desires:

1. To be free of any financial concerns (abundance of wealth)
2. To wake up every morning enthused about how you get to spend your day (abundance of passion and creativity)
3. To enjoy daily relationships with companions who are upbeat, enthusiastic, and creatively productive (abundance of a like-minded tribe)

Everything you listed will fit into one or more of those three statements. (Having fun so far?)

Now write a page of exactly what your dream looks like, and write it in present tense. Be as specific as possible. Here's an example:

> I am so happy and grateful now that I am independently wealthy (What does your bank account look like?), living in my dream home (What does your home look like and where is it situated?), surrounded by my family (Who is sitting around your table and sleeping in your bed?), and able to experience all the things in my life and world that I desire (What else have you always dreamed of?).

This is a very simple, very general example of your dream story. Yours should be specific to what you wrote on your sheet of paper. But this goal needs to be something you don't know how to achieve as of yet. If you already know how to achieve it, you are going sideways, not forward. You need to stretch yourself to grow, not just regurgitate a safe, known goal.

Now reduce this story to one or two sentences. Read it to yourself, read it aloud, and read it in front of a mirror. Write it at least five times a day, but keep it to yourself for the time being as we don't want your closest relatives to Google "how to commit a crazy person to the psychiatric ward." We will deal with them later.

It would be great to have a trusted friend on this journey, one who will understand and participate in this tomfoolery, but a beloved pet will also work.

The point is to write a statement that evokes the emotion you want to feel when you reach this goal and then actually feel the emotion in the present tense. It's the feelings, not the facts, that I want you to concentrate on.

Examples

Go general:

I am living in a gorgeous mountain home that brings me joy each morning. Not: I live at 123 Mountain Road.

I love my body, which moves and feels amazing. Not: I wear a size eight—in my dreams.

I love my partner and my family and am so blessed to share my life with them. Not: I am married to the high school hero who always ignored me.

I propose you come up with an amazing list of your desires but keep it general. Give the Universe wide latitude to fill in the specifics. It will deliver to you the most amazing objects needed to fulfill your desires and will induce those emotions you want to feel— perhaps not exactly as you predicted, but much more satisfying.

Write this succinct statement on a "goal card," and carry it with you at all times, experiencing the emotions you will feel when you arrive at that scene.

You will be amazed when you arrive at the desired destination. You will realize that you are feeling the emotions you wrote on your goal card, and that they are even better than you imagined (notice that word again, *imagined*) but perhaps quite different from what you had initially projected. Remember, there is never a finish line as your dreams keep growing, expanding, and soaring.

This now takes us back to the second part of our earlier discussion regarding why you don't know what you want to dream about because "you're happy with what you have." This represents a lack of awareness about how the universe works.

Being happy where you are *is* wonderful; in fact, it's a *requirement* for achieving your dream. It is necessary for the expansion of your universe, but it is not to be used as an excuse for staying where you are. You need to grow your happiness.

Another natural law of the universe (Law of Transmutation) states that everything is changing form and is expanding or contracting. Remember the parable of the talents where the slave who did not grow his portion ended up with nothing? It is because of this law, not because of a mean master. If you aren't expanding and growing, you are contracting and shrinking. Nothing is ever static. The same is true for you and the Universe. Nothing remains still. If you aren't growing, you are disintegrating. Let's become aware of this and learn to grow our happiness.

We accept our current state of comfort and call it happiness for three reasons:

1. We don't want to appear ungrateful.
2. We're afraid if we move from this happiness, we will crash and burn.
3. We've become catatonic to life.

(However, you must not be too catatonic or fearful because you have already decided to come on this journey with me.)

You are to be congratulated for recognizing that there is

something inside of you—a whisper, a yearning, or a gentle tug—that says, "Maybe there's more." Let's keep going, shall we?

Exercise

1. Write out the dream sentence outlined earlier. You are not risking life or limb to just start the process. As you become aware that growing is what the Universe, God, Source, or Infinite Intelligence expects of you and know it is the natural order of life and laws of the infinite, you stick your toe in the water, just a little, and experiment. You decide you want to grow the happiness you already have. You will find that the effect this increased happiness, knowledge, awareness, growth, and opportunity has—not only on you but also on your loved ones and on the environment—is enormous. It is felt in the entire cosmos.

2. Read your goal card aloud many times each day. Post a copy on your mirror, in your car, and on your computer at work. When you see this card, always feel the emotions you will experience when this dream is achieved. Start thinking about the action steps you will need to take on your journey to your goal. Start thinking different thoughts.

"I don't think of myself as a poor, deprived ghetto girl who made good. I think of myself as somebody who from an early age knew I was responsible for myself, and I had to make good."

—Oprah Winfrey

A note from the author:

Make sure you are running toward your passion, not running away from the current situation.

Before I was aware of the magic of the Universe, aware of the natural laws and the power I possessed, I yearned for something more, something different.

It was 1998. After practicing law for almost twenty years, I began to feel a sense of panic and doom. Whether it was caused by a midlife crisis, a glimpse of mortality, or just being a burned-out divorce attorney, I knew I badly wanted to change professions.

I probably should have homed in on the word *badly* and the feeling that I longed to get away from something I didn't want. I should have discovered what I truly desired.

The path I took—trying to run away from my profession and begin a new business on the side—was littered with difficulties, broken relationships, and ultimately, financial disaster.

I happened upon a new massage procedure widely used in Europe to sculpt the body. Amazingly, it worked well. I hatched an idea and convinced my husband and a friend to open a health and beauty center. I called it a medical spa. (I swear I coined the phrase.) We offered endermologie (the massage procedure), microdermabrasion, Botox, laser hair removal, massages, and facials (procedures that are now a normality but at the time almost unheard of).

The store was beautiful and peaceful, with massage chairs and a waterfall for weary customers. The concept was great, and the customers loved it, but it wasn't making enough money to replace my law income.

I *needed* more money to *run away* from my job, so what did I do? I opened a second spa in California with the help of a dear high school friend.

Now there were two sets of rent, machines, employees, supplies, and taxes. Suffice it to say, after a long series of stressful events, I couldn't keep the shops going. I had maxed out my credit cards, wiped out our retirement accounts, taken all the equity out of the house, and was dead broke.

It still wasn't enough to keep the business going, so with a broken heart and a broken spirit, I closed the spas and declared bankruptcy on the business debts.

It was humiliating. It damaged my friendships and made my family much poorer. It took me years to recover financially.

It was such a great concept. I had executed it well, and the customers loved it. So why didn't it work? It didn't work because I was trying to get away from something. I was doing it to make money. I wasn't doing it because it was my passion or my dream. There is such a tremendous lesson here for all of us. When you are setting your big, amazing goal, make sure you are doing it because of a passion for that goal. Make sure you are running toward the dream, not away from your current situation.

The Universe only works its magic when you have discovered what makes your soul sing and you start feeling the amazing emotion of love, passion, and excitement. It doesn't work when you are only doing it for the money or retreating from a situation.

Focus on what your heart wants, follow the natural laws, and believe you can achieve it. The abundance you yearn for will flow freely to you.

A few years later, I invented, trademarked, and patented a magnetic bracelet/watch that was called Counter Clock. Attached to a watch were four thin bands, each containing a magnetic bead that allowed you to track your daily, healthy activities. Each time you accomplished an activity, you moved the magnetic bead over a notch to keep track of it for the day. It was an early Fitbit before there were Fitbits.

Once again, thousands of dollars later, it came to a halt because of production costs, marketing, etc. It was a great idea before it's time, but not successful.

I wanted to replace my income, not soar to my highest ability. The doors didn't open; the magic didn't appear.

But did I stop there? Oh no. Along with another dear friend, who has stayed a dear friend, we started a reusable bag business called Sackaroos®. The bags were made of strong, washable mesh that could each hold twenty-five pounds. Eight of them could fit into a handy canvas pouch that fit in your glove compartment. We received positive national press, sold thousands of dollars' worth, and even attracted a buyer at Bed Bath & Beyond. But once again, production costs and a series of setbacks caused the enterprise to close. To this day, I continue to get requests for replacements.

Great idea, great product, but it wasn't my passion. I didn't have the emotional energy, the correct vibration, or the tenacity to continue with it. We began the company to help the environment, of course, but mostly it was to replace our incomes. It wasn't my dream.

This time we didn't lose much money. We developed and made a great product, but the enterprise failed.

At the time, I thought these were all failures. However, looking back at those situations, I realize they caused me to grow as a person.

The one reason we set goals is to grow. Remember, like the Universe, we either expand or contract.

There is no failure unless you quit. And I didn't quit. I grew.

Chapter 3

- -

Do You Believe in Magic?

"The most important question you can ever ask is, do you believe the Universe to be a friendly place?" —Albert Einstein

"Therefore, I tell you, whatever you ask for in prayer, believe that you have received it, and it will be yours." —Mark 11:24

Our belief system is the foundation for our entire life. But we are like a fish in water.

"They don't know they're in water. If you tried to explain it, they would say, 'Water, what's water?' They are so surrounded by it, it's impossible to see. They can't see it until they get outside of it," writes Derek Sivers.

Our beliefs are like the water. We have been engrossed in them so long, we think that is all there is. We can't see the "water." These beliefs have been programmed into us, even before birth. Our past conditioning and experiences create our beliefs. Our beliefs interpret our everyday life experiences. Our actions are based on how we interpret these life experiences and thus control our current situation.

Beliefs are the colored glasses through which we see the world, unaware that we have the ability to take them off or change the lenses. Everything in our lives is filtered through these beliefs, yet we don't recognize them as beliefs. We recognize them as truth.

Here are some examples that will help explain this statement: 1491—The world is flat. It looks flat. Mom told me it was flat. Leaders established it is flat. It is logical that it is flat. I believe the world is flat. That is the truth.

Spoiler alert: the earth is not flat. Your belief was inaccurate, but you weren't even aware it was up for discussion. It colored all you did and thought about the world.

1890—Man cannot fly, never could. No wings, can't get off the ground. We stay firmly on the earth to travel. It is a truth: man cannot fly.

Your imagination is limited to ground travel and the distance it takes to get to your destination. You believe there is no other way. It is obviously the truth.

1908—Women are sweet little creatures that are good mommas and wives, but surely we don't think they are smart enough to vote or own land. They can't be trusted to use their brains to make important decisions, so men must do so. It is the truth.

Heck, I can't even think of anything witty to say here except "You've come along way, baby."

Whether it is a misunderstanding of geography, aerodynamics, or cultural conditioning, at the time it was considered the truth. Period.

The same dynamics play out in your lives every day and in every action you take. You think there is only one truth, not open to debate. You accept it and trudge on through life.

Your belief system establishes your truth. However, your beliefs are based on the constant barrage of faulty information.

Information given lovingly by your parents, I'm sure. Information given unequivocally by your teachers and drummed into you by society. The information given is not necessarily truths, only the conditioning we call beliefs.

"Belief is just a thought you keep thinking." —Abraham Hicks

Here are some examples you may recognize:

- There is only so much to go around.
- You must _____ (go to college, live in a certain neighborhood, have a certain pigment in your skin color, etc.) to be successful.
- You are alone. You are separate from others.
- Someone else controls your life, future, and economy.
- You are not worthy of greatness.
- You deserve what you get.
- You are a victim and someone needs to take care of you.

What if, stay with me here, none of those statements were true—only regurgitated information passed down ad nauseam through centuries?

What if we recognize we are goldfish surrounded by these faulty conclusions? What if we become *aware* of the fact they are not true, only opinions or inaccurate findings of fact? What if I can show you scientific evidence, recently discovered, that proves these original assumptions are as flat as the ancient world?

What if we answered Einstein's question: We do believe the universe is a friendly place! Could he possibly have meant that our beliefs, the way we view the world, literally affects our universe? Yes! Yes! Yes! Yes! Yes!

Once we become aware that our beliefs are fluid and only based on past conditioning, we can decide to make a change.

It doesn't even matter if you can't define what your beliefs are. You don't need years of therapy to "peel the layers of your onion" (from Shrek, my favorite philosopher). You just need to be aware that beliefs are conditioned responses and can be modified.

Look at your life. It will be a reflection of your beliefs to date. No judgments, no regrets, no worries—just a reflection. If you don't like what you see in your life, your beliefs may not serve you. You don't have to define what you believe in at the present moment; you just need to define what you *want* to believe in.

"The outer condition of a person's life will always be found to reflect their inner beliefs." —James Allen

"We think in secret, and it comes to pass. Environment is but our looking glass." —James Allen

"Man is what he believes."
—Anton Chekhov (not to be confused with the Star Trek lieutenant)

"The moment you doubt whether you can fly, you cease forever to be able to do it." —J. M. Barrie, author of *Peter Pan*

"People only see what they are prepared to see."
—Ralph Waldo Emerson

"Man becomes what he believes himself to be. If I keep on saying to myself that I cannot do a certain thing, it is possible that I may end by really becoming incapable of doing it.

"On the contrary, if I shall have the belief I can do it, I shall surely acquire the capacity to do it, even if I may not have had the ability at the beginning." —Mahatma Gandhi

"Whether you think you can or think you can't, you are right." —Henry Ford

Starting right this second, decide what you want to believe, only what you want to see in your life. Here's a list to help you get started:

- I am worthy. I can accomplish, acquire, and become everything I can dream of and believe in.
- There is not just one pie that we are all fighting over. There are unlimited pies. Make another pie.
- I am a spiritual being having a human experience. All spirit is connected. We are all connected. Quantum physics proves this.
- I have the power and responsibility to control my environment and achieve every result I desire. No one has power or control over my thinking, believing, and achieving.

"Everything can be taken from a man but one thing: the last of human freedoms—to choose one's attitude in any given set of circumstances, to choose one's own way," wrote Viktor Frankl in *Man's Search for Meaning*. (Frankl, a Viennese psychiatrist, spent World War II in a German concentration camp.)

"Isn't it great that the above statements can be embraced, believed, and accomplished?" I exclaim.

"But so unrealistic," you reply. "It's a bunch of hocus-pocus to think I can believe these things are true and then they come to pass."

Yes, it is hocus-pocus! It is magical. It is, well, unbelievable. You believe it not to be true based on the conditioned mind-set through which you see the world. You believe me to be nuts.

And that, I reply, is why you don't see it in your life. You have been conditioned to believe the opposite.

Until you believe a new story (it's a friendly Universe controlled by the decision to see it as friendly), nothing can be called forth to allow you to achieve your dreams.

One of my favorite stories will show how a new set of beliefs can transform your life:

Monica was a hairdresser. One of her clients was a consultant in Bob Proctor's program "Thinking into Results." When she heard about the program, Monica was intrigued. She made a leap of faith and enrolled in the program. Her most precious dream was to become a best-selling author, telling the story of how she overcame obstacles in her life.

After being instructed to write a goal card with her dream on it, she started writing "I am a best-selling author" on anything that would stand still. She bought blank journals and wrote this statement hundreds of times a day, filling up one journal after another. She started to believe she could actually write a book, so she began to write the chapters.

She continued to write her goal card statement hundreds of times a day. She finished her book. She found a self-publishing company, published it, and became a best-selling Amazon author!

Her consultant was so impressed that he hired her to be a salesperson for his business and help enroll others who also wanted to achieve their dreams.

She then became so proficient at her job that she came to the attention of Bob Proctor. He hired her to be one of his salespeople. Her career and income soared.

All because she started to believe her life could be different and her dream could become a reality.

The clients who work personally with me also have amazing stories: a salesperson tripled her sales after taking the class; another found her dream job; and a third started a new business, which is now booming. Others have found the love of their life, adopted that longed-for baby, changed careers, and expanded all areas of their lives. They all learned to change what they believed could happen.

"The world we see that seems so insane is the result of a belief system that is not working. To perceive the world differently, we must be willing to change our belief system, let the past slip away, expand our sense of now, and dissolve the fear in our minds."

—William James

"The thing always happens that you really believe in and the belief in a thing makes it happen." —Frank Lloyd Wright

You can never change your life unless you first change your beliefs to better serve you. And I am talking about embracing a deep, down-to-your-core belief, not just paying lip service to it. Let's just say, for grins, that you do want an abundant, healthy life doing what you dream of doing. How do you go about changing the conditioning that has created your beliefs, especially when these beliefs are not obvious?

1. Decide on an amazing dream (chapter 2).
2. Understand abundance is real and necessary in your life (chapter 1).
3. Comprehend your beliefs are not absolute truths, only conditioned responses (chapter 3).

Deepak Chopra writes, "A belief is the blueprint, but you are the builder. The dreams only become a reality when you pick up the hammer and start building. But a step before that, before the dream, is your belief. If you don't believe something can happen, you can't even get to the dream stage."

All the concepts we are learning swirl together. You should begin to see by now that you can only dream based on your current beliefs, your current limitations. You need to change your beliefs first to open the dream catalog. However, you must desire a bigger dream before you can decide to change your belief system. You must become *aware* that something more is possible before you can change your beliefs, but your current beliefs stop you from seeing that something more is possible.

Okay, I'm dizzy.

You are becoming aware that there is a different way to view your world. That's enough for right now. The picture starts to emerge when you attain more pieces of the puzzle.

Our awareness spirals up. We look at something we wish to achieve, which is just out of reach, based on our current belief system. We use the proven steps to obtain this desire, and from that vantage point, we can set a new goal based on a new belief. We begin to internalize this new belief, and we start seeing the world through a new set of beliefs. We then begin to encounter new coincidences and our beliefs, our goals, our actions, and our results spiral up.

"Seeing is not believing, believing is seeing. You see things, not as they are, but as you are," wrote author and minister Eric Butterworth.

You have to change *you*, your subconscious mind, to see the new opportunities around you. You begin to believe a little more is possible as more opportunities become visible that had not been there before (doors appear that once were just walls). The opportunities have always been there; you just needed a different perspective, a different set of lenses to view them.

Our best-selling author, Monica, had no idea that her dream would become a reality. She did what she was told, internalized a new belief, and started taking baby steps one at a time. Soon doors that once were walls started opening. She changed her beliefs and had faith in the process.

You should now have a little more faith that "this stuff works" (my husband's favorite saying). You can see a little further down the road and dream a bigger dream based on your new belief system. The new belief is getting easier to imagine because you acknowledge it has worked for smaller things. You are now open to more of the serendipities of life. You see even more results. Your life spirals up. You choose to set new goals, to grow, to "feed the good wolf."

There is an old Indian legend: The elder chief explains to the young braves that there are two wolves fighting inside of them: a good wolf and a bad wolf. "Which will win?" ask the boys. "The one you feed," answers the wise man.

Excerpt from my daily journal:

"So how do we know what our beliefs are? I think I know what I believe, but the truth lies in what I see reflected in my life. And if we have beliefs that might not serve us (scarcity, fear of failure), how do we change them? My beliefs enhance my life, not distract from it. So, I hone my beliefs, write my beliefs, and concentrate on these new beliefs.

"We have control over our thoughts and actions. These can be positive, such as having compassion for ourselves and others, being a good steward of our earth (especially our little piece of it), and trusting in ourselves. Stay in the moment, and choose wisely. Choose a new thought, smile at a stranger, hold open a door, leave a bigger tip, or write a kind note to someone. Become more aware of your options in each moment. Always feed your good wolf; eat healthy food, read good books, have only positive screen time, exercise, write in cursive, meditate, take care of your stuff, get rid of the clutter. Have faith that the good wolf will win the fight and lead you to the stars!"

Exercises

1. What do you want to believe? Be specific. Examples: I believe I am successful. I believe I have a beautiful, healthy body. I believe I can have everything I truly want. I believe people are good. I believe the world is getting better and better. Keep going.

2. Think of a time in your past when you believed something different would happen—perhaps outside of what you thought was possible at the time—and it did. You got that great job, you were accepted into that great school, you found that new "somebody." Was that wishing or believing? What does it feel like when you *wish* for something? What does it feel like when you *believe* in something? Feel the difference: wishing is hoping while believing is knowing.

Chapter 4

- -

The Secret of The Secret

We have journeyed from the first chapter that told us abundance is not only an option but also necessary and accessible by all. It is literally a requirement to be able to live a most authentic, productive, talented, and joyful life.

We learned that everyone defines abundance differently but always includes everything necessary to develop, grow, and expand.

We heard from ancient and contemporary masters who espoused we must acknowledge the abundance the universe offers and continually avail ourselves of this infinite supply, or we are not living up to our divine heritage.

We then discussed setting amazing goals based on individual desires and dreams. We discovered some exercises to help uncover these long-hidden yearnings. We began to define what the life of our dreams looks like. We again shared quotes from teachers regarding the fact that growing is an integral part of this universe. It is a natural law that we must expand, or we disintegrate.

And I can tell by the look in your eye you are having none of it.

"I've read these sorts of books before," you tell me. "I've seen 'The Secret' sixty-four times and written and read and said affirmations until I'm blue.

"I obviously want this information to be real, or I wouldn't have once again purchased a book that hints at a different, more exciting and fulfilling life. But I'm baffled at why this doesn't work for me. Unless you can offer something that is missing from the other self-help books out there, I'm checking out and heading for the cookies."

Stop right there, and put the Oreos down. As it just so happens, I can offer the missing link. I am fortunate to have been introduced to the exact mentors I needed at the exact time to explain this missing link.

For the introduction and the joy this concept of magical thinking brings, the Universe brought me Mike Dooley. And when I needed to go deeper and find out why these amazing concepts work, I serendipitously stumbled upon Bob Proctor and the answers.

I hope I may act as a mentor for you and show you why some books may have not worked for you in the past and then offer action steps you can take to activate the magic in your life.

The secret lies within Joe Somebody. It also lies within me and what I thought was expected and necessary to lead a successful life. It lies within you too.

The secret is the past conditioning, or paradigms, that we have been exposed to throughout our lives and that control our lives 95 percent of the time.

Your current beliefs are shaped by your paradigms and past conditioning. (Paradigms are a multitude of habits instilled in your subconscious mind.) If you don't have the life of your dreams, it is only because you don't believe you can have it. You don't believe you can have it, because if you did, you wouldn't be reading this book—you'd already be living the life of your dreams.

Our past conditioning is not usually something that we have chosen or are even aware of. It was probably not even consciously passed on by our parents, teachers, schools, etc., as they were also programmed by others. And although it is not our fault, once we become aware of it, we have the power and responsibility to select a new set of paradigms of our choosing. Let me explain.

Assume for a moment that *belief* is the foundation for attracting to you all that you desire. Without actual belief, to-the-very-core-of-your-being belief, none of this hocus-pocus works.

How do you change your belief system? We first need to look at how our mind works. With knowledge comes power. And this is powerful stuff.

I want to share the story of how this information has become available to me and many others.

Bob Proctor—the multimillionaire chairman of a globally respected institute, my mentor and developer of this organized information—started out a mess. He had only two months—yes, months—of high school. He was a very poor student, a very poor reader. He was also a very poor employee, and he lost many jobs. When he was twenty-six, he finally landed his dream job as a fireman in Toronto. He was making $4,000 a year. However, because of his unsuccessful past, he owed $6,000. Now that may not seem like a lot by today's standards, but assume you owed 150 percent of your yearly salary. It would seem overwhelming to you, as it did to Bob.

One day he was lamenting about this great debt, as it was always on his mind, when a friend handed him a book and told him to read it and do exactly as it said. The short version is he did just that. The long version is it took many conversations and suggestions from his friend for Bob to do just that. He said he couldn't read well. He said he didn't believe it would work. He said he didn't have time. But the friend persisted. Bob read it. And read it. And read it. And read it. And within one year, he was making over $175,000—a (let me get my calculator out) 4,300 percent increase. In one year. (*The ABCs of Success*, Bob Procter, TarcherPerigee, 2015.)

And what was the book he read? The iconic business treatise *Think and Grow Rich* by Napoleon Hill. This classic book was published in 1938 after twenty-five years of research. Since that time, it has made millions of millionaires.

It is worth a paragraph to share the book's rich history. In 1908, Andrew Carnegie was the wealthiest man in the world. A cub reporter by the name of Napoleon Hill was assigned to spend three hours interviewing Carnegie for an article. The three hours turned into three days as the men immediately became friends. At the end of that time, Carnegie offered Hill a proposal. Although Carnegie was wealthy and already a generous philanthropist, he wanted to leave more of a legacy. He wanted to find out why he became so successful and leave this information for the ages. Because he didn't know the answer, he asked Hill to make a commitment to discover the "recipe for success." Carnegie would introduce him to all the wealthy and successful people in the world, allowing Hill to interview them, and Hill would find the common denominator they all possessed.

Hill would do this without any remuneration from Carnegie.

He accepted this challenge, and for the next twenty-five years, he interviewed five hundred of the world's most successful individuals.

The information he obtained was succinctly organized into specific characteristics all of the interviewed people shared. Hill had discovered the recipe for success and shared it in his book *Think and Grow Rich*. The rest is history.

Fast-forward to Bob.

"After reading this book for a year, my income went from $4,000 yearly to over $175,000 a year by opening a floor-cleaning business. After five years of continually reading it, my business was now a multimillion-dollar company operating in three countries," he wrote in *The ABCs of Success*.

He thought it was the book. He bought the book for his friends, but nothing happened to improve their lives. He purchased a recording of this material and listened to it constantly. He bought the record for his friends, and still nothing happened for them. He was curious about why he became successful after reading this book while others who read it did not. He decided to dedicate his life to finding the answer. And he has. Dedicated his life. Found the answer.

The answer Bob discovered is that he literally changed his paradigms from *failing* to *succeeding*. He discovered how this feat had been accomplished and why it worked. He has shared this with millions of people. I now share it with you.

Our mind, it seems, is miraculous. Our mind is made up of two parts: the conscious mind and the subconscious mind. (This should not be confused with the brain. The brain is a physical organ, a switching station, a computer that our consciousness controls.) Our mind is our life-ness, our spirituality; it is in every cell of our body. It is eternal.

When we are born into this physical plane and forget our infinite divinity, we must then learn how to exist in this reality. And for the first six years or so, our brain is open to all of the information coming into it. Young children spend most of their time in alpha or theta brain wave cycles. (This is the same cycle people are in when they are in hypnosis.) Because they are in these brain waves, children are more open to suggestion, are in a super-learning state, and are more easily programmed by their environment.

Childhood is the time when the vast amount of our programming—our paradigms—is acquired. It shapes our conditionings. It is hardwired into our brain. It has been internalized into our subconscious mind.

Since our subconscious mind controls what we do 95 percent of our lives, it is the autopilot of our days. Our subconscious mind (which is made up by numerous paradigms) dictates our habits, our likes, and our dislikes. It controls our decisions, our dreams, and especially our beliefs.

You think what you believe is based on truth. But actually, what you *believe* is literally based on a pattern of "constant repetition of an idea" until it is internalized into your subconscious mind (our past conditioning). Think of the truth in 1491: the world was flat. A truth at the time, it is not a truth in reality. This is the same with all our belief systems. The system is made up of programmed information through which you view your personal world. It is the rose-colored, or gray-colored, or "I'm ugly and unworthy" colored glasses we see life through. It is only a statement, or thought, that was repeated so many times it has been internalized in our subconscious mind. It is not the truth; it is a habit, a way of thinking.

You can never do or be anything more than your set of beliefs allows you to do or be. You can, however, choose new beliefs, ones that will serve you. You can learn how to reprogram that subconscious mind into a new autopilot for your life.

If you have been preconditioned to think (know) …

That there is scarcity and lack in this world,

That you are not worthy to receive abundance,

That there is only so much to go around,

That you are selfish if you want more,

That you must work hard to make a little money,

That you must trade your time for money,

Well, then you become Joe Somebody.

What if there is another way? What if you don't pick that Penalties envelope? What if you decide to choose envelope number one, Riches, and take control of your mind?

Well, that is where the magic begins. This is the secret of *The Secret*. To be fair, this is exactly why other amazing New Thought teachers encourage us to do affirmations and visualization, even if they don't know the science behind it. However, the information contained herein is a shortcut and a quantum leap forward to claiming that new, desirable life. Instead of years of doing actions that over time may or may not change that conditioning, what if we could do it in months, or even weeks?

Well, Bob Proctor found that shortcut, and he shares it with everyone. I am fortunate you have allowed me to share it with you. It's called the "stick person." What? Like in hangman? Yes, like that.

In 1934, Dr. Thurmond Fleet, a pioneer in the healing arts, wrote about the workings of the mind.

The brain thinks in pictures. When you hear the word *cat*, a picture of a cat pops up. When we try to understand the mind and begin speaking of it, we need a picture of the mind.

Since the mind is not an object but a process and an activity (not to be confused with the brain, which is an organ), there is not a picture of the mind. However, to discuss different aspects of the mind, we must have a picture of it to better understand it. Although Dr. Fleet created a diagram in 1934, I created my own based on his groundbreaking ideas, updated for the twenty-first century. The following is my rendition of the stick person that gives us a picture of the mind so we may discuss it and begin to understand its amazing power.

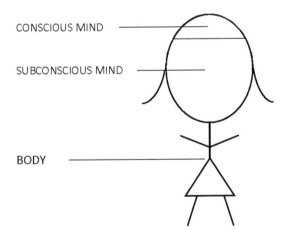

CONSCIOUS MIND

SUBCONSCIOUS MIND

BODY

Let the top part of the circle represent your conscious mind, which controls what we do 5 percent of our day. Let the bottom part represent the subconscious mind, the 95 percent of our day that is on autopilot. Let the small triangle represent our body. The body is small because our physicality has little to do with how we learn to make huge changes in our lives.

Our conscious mind is our intellectual mind, our learning mind. We can choose what we put into it. It can accept or reject what it is exposed to. It is where we store our lessons from school, information from books, everyday knowledge, etc. The conscious mind, since it is capable of choice, allows us to choose a new set of ideas that we wish to program into our lives. But when the new information only resides in the conscious mind, it does not change our programming.

The conscious mind only controls what we do 5 percent of our day. We can never expect to have enough willpower derived from this 5 percent to make any substantive, permanent changes. It is not possible. We must learn how to program new information into our subconscious mind.

Our subconscious mind is our emotional mind. This is where our programming resides. It cannot reject; it can only accept what is programmed into it. It controls our body, our emotions, our actions, our reactions, and our results. It controls our behavior and our lives 95 percent of the time. And the program it is running is as old as a floppy disk that was inputted decades ago. It is time to upgrade.

It is simple, it is free, and it is open to all. But you must become *aware* of how to do it and be motivated by your dreams to stay committed to the process.

There are only two ways to change the paradigms, our subconscious mind.

One is an intense, emotional impact. Such experiences are extremely out of the ordinary. They immediately change our belief about a situation. A near-death experience or the sudden death of a loved one are some examples. September 11 was also such an event. This kind of event is usually negative.

The second way to reprogram your subconscious mind is to

choose a new thought or belief to replace an old paradigm. You accomplish this reprogramming by thinking this new thought with constant, spaced repetition of this new idea with a strong emotion.

Take your goal statement from chapter 2, read it, write it, and think about it several times a day. Imagine it is reality. Visualize yourself with that desire. Do this often, with strong emotions, and you will soon have a shiny new paradigm of your own choosing that now controls 95 percent of that aspect of your life.

It becomes so easy once this new idea is internalized. You are now operating from this new paradigm, and your actions become almost effortless. Your life is now on an autopilot of your choosing. You are floating down stream, no longer fighting the current.

Your subconscious mind also dictates your self-image. Your self-image—your belief in who you are and what you are capable of accomplishing—has been programmed by your paradigms.

Your self-image is set just as a thermostat is set. If your life strays from this self-image (as a thermostat might stray from a preprogrammed temperature because a window is open), your subconscious mind kicks in to bring it back to the preset image of yourself (just as a heater will kick on to bring the temperature back to the prearranged setting). Your subconscious mind will constantly bring you back to your self-image paradigm.

Until it is changed, the subconscious mind will continue to reinforce your self-image based on past programming.

How does our subconscious mind control our life so completely? There are billions of bits of information in our environment available each second. Most of this information is beyond our current ability to access—dog whistles, ultraviolet light, microwaves, etc. Our subconscious mind can access about two thousand bits each second. Out of those two thousand bits of information it has access to, it chooses about fifty bits of information that are consistent with your paradigms and feeds you just those bits—only that information, none of the other.

These are the things in your environment that you are aware of and are reacting to. You think it is the only information available. It is, however, the only information that your paradigm allows you to see. You do not see the other 1,950 bits. You think your world is flat.

There is story about the Native Americans who first greeted Columbus. They asked these new visitors where they had come from. When the sailors pointed toward the huge ships anchored in the water offshore, however, the Native Americans couldn't see the ships. It was not in their conditioning that something so large was possible. It wasn't in their "wheelhouse." It wasn't until they recognized that something was interfering with the tide and traced the water back to the ships affecting it, that they could comprehend the unusual sight. The ships were not contained in the fifty bits of information the natives were receiving from their subconscious mind.

We can only observe what we are programmed to see. If you have been programmed to believe there is scarcity, only information relating to that condition is fed to you by your subconscious.

"But there is only scarcity," you cry. "Am I to deny reality?"

It is not reality. It is only your current bits of information of reality. Your amazing subconscious mind is conditioned to show you only what the program allows it to. It brings you right back to your paradigm, to where your thermostat is set.

If you think or believe (programmed) that you are ugly, that is all your subconscious mind will show you. (You will see your big nose, not your gorgeous eyes.) If you have been told your entire life you are beautiful, and that a large nose is wonderful, you will see beauty.

If you are a conservative, you will only notice things that correspond with your programmed view. If you are a liberal, you will never notice the conservative information and only access what you believe. No wonder we all can't get along.

If you believe you are fat and want to lose weight, your subconscious mind will struggle with you and keep you at that weight because that is what you believe. It is programmed to succeed (continue the program) by reflecting back to your beliefs. If you lose ten pounds, your subconscious mind will find a way to put it back on. This is the reason the vast majority of people never keep their weight off. You can't fight with only 5 percent of your mind. You need new conditioning. You need reinforcements. You need the subconscious mind to bring in the cavalry.

Let's look at lottery winners. Statistics show that at least 85 percent of the people who win the lottery file bankruptcy within five years. They are programmed for lack, poverty, or the "just making it" mentality. As long as the winners continue to be programmed this way, their subconscious mind will get them right back to where they are programmed: dead broke.

It is virtually impossible to change these paradigms, and therefore your opinions and beliefs, by only using your conscious mind. (Remember, your beliefs are the cornerstone for all this magic to work.) Even if you use what is termed "willpower" during the 5 percent of your day that you have any control over, you cannot change your paradigms.

But you can choose to use the 5 percent of your day you do have control over and learn how to pick a new thought—one that serves you. You can learn to internalize this new thought to such a degree that it replaces the negative paradigm. Your subconscious mind will then sift through those two thousand bits of "reality" and begin to show you "new" information, which was always available but not in harmony with your former paradigms.

This is where the coincidences and serendipities appear. You think, "What a coincidence I happened to be in that place at that time to have that amazing new thing happen". The fact is your subconscious mind is showing you different information. The information was always there. You are now paying attention to a different reality because your autopilot is showing you a different set of bits.

Your life begins to change. New options appear. You now start to believe this sh%# works. Pay attention to that word *belief.* Your life and dreams start to spiral up. Your world starts expanding as your subconscious mind is focused on different bits of information.

You must believe it to see it, not the other way around. And just *saying* you believe a certain way does not fool that cunning subconscious mind. Your paradigms keep you from believing what you *wish* you could believe when you are not programmed that way.

There is a way around that conundrum, however. Your subconscious mind does not know the difference between real and imagined emotion. Belief is just an emotion.

Think about going to a horror movie and being frightened. You may consciously know the fear is not based in fact, but the fear you feel is an emotion, and your subconscious mind only recognizes the emotion—not the reason behind it. It kicks the body into gear. Your heart rate increases, adrenaline pumps quickly into your body, and you become engaged in a fight–or–flight reaction. Your body is in a vibration of fear and is reacting to the emotion that your subconscious mind recognized. Remember, the subconscious mind can only accept what is put into it; it can't choose as the conscious mind can. It cannot reject this emotion. It must react according to the feeling.

We can use this to our advantage. Our thoughts produce an emotion that creates a vibration in the body. We can choose a new thought, which produces a new emotion, which in turn creates a new vibration. We can choose to vibrate differently. Let me explain why this is important.

We live in a vibrational universe. Everything vibrates at a subatomic level.

"Everything is energy, and that's all there is to it. Match the frequency of the reality you want, and you cannot help but get that reality. It can be no other way. This is not philosophy; this is physics," wrote Albert Einstein.

A rock vibrates at a different frequency from water. A tree vibrates at a different frequency from mashed potatoes. Everything in the universe vibrates at a preordained frequency except for human beings. We can choose to vibrate at a different frequency. Isn't that amazing?

Emotions are words we give to the feeling we recognize when our body is vibrating at a certain level. Choose a new emotion; choose a new vibration.

The subconscious mind is the emotional mind. It is the feeling mind. When the conscious mind chooses a thought (or doesn't *choose* a thought but allows outside influences to cause a thought), this thought produces a vibration based on past programming. The vibration is recognized as a certain feeling, and we have given words to each vibration, calling them *emotion*. When we "feel" anger, we recognize the vibration our body is in as a reaction to something we deem negative, and we call it *anger*. We are recognizing the vibration that the thought has triggered. Different vibrations have different names. They range from numbness to gratitude, which, by the way, is the highest vibration we can achieve.

Our thoughts produce an emotion (a specific vibration), which the subconscious mind then interprets. This interpretation causes a reaction by the body, producing the behavior. The behavior is a reaction to the thought, which causes a response by the Universe. Change the thoughts, change the vibration, and change the results.

We can change our vibrations by choosing to take control of our thoughts. Now remember that the subconscious mind doesn't know the difference between real and imagined emotions. When we choose new thoughts—and imagine a new emotion when we think those thoughts—we change our vibration. (I am skinny and rich now! I feel free and abundant and secure and sexy and powerful now!)

Imagine the feelings of happiness and gratitude you will feel when your dreams become reality, when you actually experience them in the present moment. Imagine the freedom that comes with abundance, the satisfaction that follows a huge accomplishment, and the intense love when cuddled with your soul mate. Wallow in those feelings for as long as possible. When you do, you're hoodwinking that subconscious mind into recognizing these new emotions of happiness, joy, and satisfaction you are feeling in the present moment. It is now vibrating in these new frequencies because you are literally feeling them. Because it is vibrating in a different frequency (remember, the subconscious mind cannot tell the difference between real and imagined emotion), it begins to show you different bits of information in your environment. When this happens, you react differently. The Universe responds in kind.

"By golly, I think you've got it."

"The Universe is not punishing you or blessing you. The Universe is responding to the vibrational attitude that you are emitting." —Abraham Hicks

When we do this often with this imagined emotion, we begin to create a new program, new paradigms, and new results. With this new programming come the new bits of information being fed consistently to us by the subconscious mind, resulting in new experiences, new options, and new behavior.

We have changed the "soil" that our dreams grow in. The environment in which we choose to plant the seeds of our utmost desires is now conducive to allowing them to grow effortlessly like a small acorn in a fertile plant bed that effortlessly produces a mighty oak.

I realized how much my emotions really do affect the outside environment while practicing an experiment I use in my classes.

From the book *E-Squared*, by Pam Grout (one of my absolute favorite authors), the experiment requires two metal hangers from the closet. The hangers should be bent in an *L* shape with the handle five inches long and the barrel approximately eleven inches long. A straw (from any fast-food restaurant) is cut in half and slipped over each handle.

When you hold the two hangers at heart level, about six inches away from your body, and think positive thoughts, the hangers move away from the body. (Positive electromagnetic currents from the heart push the metal wires forward.) When you think negative thoughts, the negative currents pull the metal piece toward the heart. (It really works; you've got to try it!)

When practicing this at home, I was totally amazed with the result. I called for my son to try the wands. He was nineteen at the time and, suffice it to say, was not on the "path" I wanted for him. I was always waiting for the other shoe to fall.

As he came toward me, the metal hangers turned inward quickly. I didn't move them; the electromagnetic current in my heart was emitting negative emotions. I was shocked. I was not even consciously thinking about his past shenanigans. I realized then how much negative emotion I was feeling.

I decided my negative emotion was going to stop. I began to mentally send him love whenever I thought about it. I hugged him when he walked across the room. Initially he was resistant, but he soon sought me out for hugs. I texted him cute (well, I thought they were cute), funny, and kind things all day. I made a point to hear his views. I spent some time with him each day. We made plans to do more things together. Whatever I could do to send him love, I did.

The results were dramatic to say the least. His attitude changed. His behavior changed. He was no longer defensive. He became helpful and appreciative.

When I changed my paradigm, I changed my emotions and thus my vibrations. This in turn changed the vibration my son felt from me. When he felt loved, he returned love. It continues to this day.

Exercises

Try these ways to internalize new thoughts into your subconscious mind:

1. Take that dream you now possess and have written down, and review it. "I am so happy and grateful now that I am_____." Read it, write it, and feel it as many times a day as possible.

2. What action steps can you take toward this goal every day? Keep it top of mind as much as possible. Start doing what you will do when you accomplish the dream. Window shop at expensive stores. Test-drive a Tesla. Visit open houses in the neighborhoods where you wish to live. Start writing that book. Exercise. Learn to cook healthy. Get your passport. Join a travel club. Enroll in a class. Do research on what actions steps successful people take.

Start doing, or at least start visualizing yourself doing all of the above.

3. Take ten minutes a day and imagine (visualize) you have that goal and feel the emotion.

4. Read books on the subject. Make friends with people in this community. Go to seminars, workshop, or retreats of your favorite authors (Pick me! Pick me!). Constantly do things that convince your subconscious mind that you have already arrived. Feed the good wolf!

This will change the thermostat in that autopilot of the mind, and you will finally be cool (not that you weren't already)!

Here's another exercise you can do, also from Pam Grout's book. It's a great example of the serendipity I found after I instructed my mind to look for a specific "bit" of information.

The book indicated you should ask the Universe to show you something specific within the next twenty-four hours. The request must be something that, when it happens, you cannot help but know the Universe sent it to you.

In the paragraph following Pam's instructions was the word *cacophony*. As I couldn't remember what the word meant, I looked up the definition: "din, racket, discord, uproar." I decided the Universe would show me that word again in the next twenty-four hours.

Hours passed. No cacophony.

The next day I was driving to Colorado, and I was attempting to listen to an Audible book. I couldn't access it, so I pulled over at the next exit.

I typed an email to the Audible site: "My account isn't working." I hit "send," and the autocorrect changed the word *account* to *cacophony*. No, I am not kidding. I glanced at the time. Ten minutes left of the twenty-four-hour period. That old Universe just winked at me.

Chapter 5

Thoughts Become Things

"We become what we think about." —Buddha

We realize abundance is our birthright. We tap into a dream we uncovered that had been hidden under layers of conditioning. We understand our beliefs are the foundation from which all things begin, and we learn how to reprogram new beliefs that serve our passion more fully.

It's all fine and good when you are perusing this book, but how can we implement them daily, hourly, moment to moment?

To be able to use this information to change our lives, we need a new way of thinking, of responding to our environment, of creating and living our lives from the inside out. We need to stop reacting to outside stimuli. We need to stop living our lives from the outside in.

"When it becomes obvious goals can't be reached, adjust the action, not the goals." —Confucius

There is a space between viewing outside stimuli and reacting to it. Our five senses are programmed to react immediately to these outside stimuli; indeed, these instincts are sometimes necessary for our survival.

If we see an object hurdling toward us, we duck. If we smell smoke, we retreat. If we feel heat, we pull our hand back. Our very future could rest on how quickly we react to outside danger. When there's no time to debate, we react. If we are in danger, our instinct and senses are handy to have.

However, absent a saber-toothed tiger, living this way makes us feel like a pinball machine. We let outside conditions flip us one way or the other. We flip our emotions from fear to delight based on what is in front of us at the time: "Squirrel!"

We let outside conditions dictate what we think, which in turn produces what we feel. We live from the outside in, giving away our power to create our lives. We can either react to outside stimuli using our instincts, or we can learn to choose a different way to *respond* to the same stimuli, using our intellectual faculties, which in turn allows us to take control of our lives from the inside out.

The film *Groundhog Day*, starring Bill Murray, is such a perfect example of this concept. For those of you who haven't seen it a zillion times, let me quickly review.

Phil Connors (Murray) is an unhappy, snarky, weatherman sent to Punxsutawney, Pennsylvania, to cover the annual Groundhog Day festivities. Because of a snowstorm, he must spend the night. For some unknown reason perpetuated by some unknown force, he awakens the day after the event to realize it is still Groundhog Day. Because he is an unhappy, snarky person, he continues to be extremely obnoxious, making himself and others miserable as he goes about his day.

This situation goes on forever, it seems. Each day is Groundhog Day, and each day he encounters the same people, doing and saying the same things. And he reacts the same way: deplorable.

Connors becomes so depressed by this hamster wheel of life (ring any bells?) that he tries desperately to get out of the situation. He steals cars, robs banks, and finally commits suicide, only to find out the next morning that he is still alive and still in Pennsylvania—and it's still Groundhog Day, over and over and over again (sound familiar?).

This continues until he decides to *think* differently. He decides to appreciate what he does have and to respond differently to the same situation he had encountered many times before. He makes friends, learns to play the piano and speak French, reads classical literature, shows compassion for a homeless man, changes a tire, and even catches a boy falling from a tree. Nothing in his environment changes except one thing: he changes. He chooses to think a different thought and to respond a different way to outside stimuli. He chooses to feed the good wolf.

He changes himself from the inside out, and then the outside miraculously changes before his eyes. He has become authentic. He has found genuine abundance. In a small town, with the same people and with limited resources, he chose a different thought and a different way to view the only reality he had. And when he did, the "long winter, bleak and dark, bereft of hope" ends, and he finally wakes up to a new day—literally, February 3.

Connors had to make peace with himself, he had to appreciate all he possessed in the moment, and he had to grow and expand, even in that limited environment. And when he did, he realized, like Dorothy in Oz, he'd "had it all along."

We all have that choice in whatever environment we find ourselves. But first we need to learn how to do it, how to find that different path.

The different path consists of learning to *respond* to the outside world. Instead of a knee-jerk reaction to a situation using our five physical senses and based on past conditioning (example: if the word *tiger* triggers fear, you immediately run; if the word reminds you of a cartoon character bouncing on his tail, you look for Piglet), we can choose to respond to that situation using our intellectual faculties.

In that "space" we initially talked about, between observing a situation and reacting, what if we could choose a different mindset? What if we could become more aware of that space, expand it, take inventory of the amazing God-given tools we have (but rarely take out of the tool box), and choose a different way to respond? Not out of immediacy or unconsciousness but out of a deliberate intent to create a response that serves our goal and dream. (Incidentally, I just spilled coffee on my white carpet and blurted out an expletive. Sometimes you just have to react.)

These tools are the six intellectual faculties we all possess that allow us to consciously respond to the outside world. When used consistently and deliberately, we take control of our lives and live from the inside out.

The intellectual faculties are will, imagination, memory, perception, intuition, and reason. My acronym for them is WIMPIR (understanding I've misspelled the word referring to a moan, but it's easy to remember).

Let's take an event and illustrate how each one works:

Someone has pulled in front of you in traffic. When you *react*—horn blaring, middle finger waving, teeth clenched—your adrenalin begins to pump, you heart rate goes up, and you are angry for the next two hours. You arrive at work upset, are snippy with the receptionist, and lose your temper with your client.

You have allowed something outside of yourself to take control of how you react and feel, and it affects your life.

Now let's choose a different way to view the same incident and choose to *respond* (space between the dumb a** cutting you off and your response), using our six intellectual facilities (WIMPIR):

Will: "I have a bigger plan for my day, and I have enough self- discipline to choose not to get angry."

Imagination: "Perhaps the few seconds longer I sit here will save me from a terrible fate."

Memory: "Boy, I remember I've done that before when I was late; now I know how the other person felt."

Perception: "I should try to look at this a different way. No one was injured, and the world is still turning." (This uses the law of relativity.)

Intuition: "I thought he might pull out so I braked a second before, and I feel grateful I did."

Reason: "The traffic is very heavy, and I couldn't have moved very far anyway, so I haven't lost much time at all."

You have just claimed your power and stayed the course to your intended goal that day, not allowing an outside source to affect it.

The more you do this, the easier it gets. The trick, of course, is to become aware that it is even possible and then expand that space—that split second—to make a different choice.

When you do this consistently, you start to see different paths appearing that you didn't know existed. When you respond differently, people respond differently to you. They may give you a lead, offer you a smile, or even become a friend. Events that seemed like obstacles become advantages. Quite simply, how you choose to respond makes all the difference in the world.

"Response-ability is the ability to choose our response to any circumstance or condition," according to leadership authority Stephen Covey. And when you respond with a positive intent, the positivity comes back to you.

"For every action, there is an equal and opposite reaction."
—Sir Isaac Newton's third law of motion

"What you sow, so shall you reap." —Galatians 6:8

The Universe gives us back what we put out. It's the action on our part that causes the reaction on the part of the Source.

When we claim our dreams, take response-ability for our actions, set our intentions, and take action on a daily basis, our lives expand dramatically. We choose not to let outside circumstances deter us from our goal. We keep our purpose front and center, and we choose to constantly respond with WIMPIR. When we continue to do this often, our lives begin to move toward our desired goal.

"Okay," you say, "I've got the general idea of responding to life—I'm kind of excited—but not a clue on what route to take to reach my dream."

Luckily, the Universe is the ultimate GPS system. All you do is input your destination (your goal) and the GPS-on-steroids will guide you there. Honest. No lie. Guaranteed.

There is one small caveat, however, when using the "Universal GPS": You must put the car into gear and literally move a little before the nice GPS lady directs your trip. You can't just sit in the driveway and tap the device, trying to make it work while you aren't moving. You must accelerate and take some action steps, even baby steps, to get this party started.

Any action with genuine intent will do. Once you put your life in gear and take action toward your dream, the Universe will show you the next step. Even if you are headed in the wrong direction, that little voice will come on and say, "Make a legal U-turn at the next available opportunity."

You can never get lost, you can never get it wrong, and you can never get it done. We are always moving, one step at a time. "You don't need to see the whole staircase, just the next step," said Martin Luther King Jr.

When you learn to trust the Universe and carve out that space to respond to life, your WIMPIR factors kick into high gear. Using your intuition, you turn the correct way. Coincidences appear; opportunities present themselves. You meet the exact people you are supposed to meet.

Using your imagination, you think of a new way to create a needed object or solution. Using your memory, an idea resurfaces. Using your reasoning, you discover a logical progression. Using your will, you soldier through.

Two more concepts are needed, however, to hone this newfound power:

1. The ability to stay in the now (chapter 6)
2. The ability to quiet your mind (chapter 7)

Exercises

1. Think of your day. Was there anything that upset you or increased your level of frustration? Write it down in detail.
2. Now take that same situation and determine how WIMPIR might have helped you respond more positively. Taking each intellectual facility separately, apply them to that specific circumstance.

Will: "Using willpower, what could I have done to use self-discipline to choose a new way to respond (not lose my temper)?"

Imagination: "I need to think outside the box, to be creative in coming up with a different way to respond. Maybe we could combine two ideas."

Memory: "Now that I think of it, I remember a time that we used this other method to solve the problem."

Perception: "Let me take a step back for a minute and see if I can look at this from a different point of view. What does the other side think?"

Intuition: "Boy, I just knew that was going to blow up. Next time I will take a second and listen to that still small voice."

Reason: "Okay, now I see why that didn't work. If I just put my mind to work, I can figure out what would."

Chapter 6

- -

Living in the Now

"The secret for both mind and body is not to mourn for the past, worry about the future, or anticipate trouble, but to live in the present moment wisely and earnestly." —Buddha

A topic that doesn't come up much outside of new age workshops— living in the present moment—is essential to claiming our genuine abundance.

For most of us, we use the precious present moment in these ways:

- Fret about the past
- Worry about the future
- Make a mental shopping list
- Become catatonic from devices.

When I was a little girl, after spending the night with my grandparents, I would run downstairs in the morning. More often than not, hundreds of rainbows would be all over the living room walls, ceiling, and floor. I asked my grandmother why she had rainbows. She answered that it was a happy house, conveniently leaving out the fact that the east-facing front door had cut glass surrounding it, causing the light to refract.

Years later, when I discovered this magical trick, I placed a cut-glass crystal in an east window, where it still resides today. Each morning I stumble to the kitchen past the window with the dangling glass ball for that first cup of coffee. Most of the time there are dozens of rainbows adorning the room. But sometimes I am so grumpy or myopic or fixated on the day, I don't pay attention to my surroundings. I miss the rainbows. I miss the "Now." They are always present. I, however, am not.

We need to be "now warriors." We need to grab it, claim it, and live it. It's all we ever have. It's our only true connection to actions, to hugs, to our dreams, and to divinity. Most of us are not "now warriors." Most of us are simply worriers.

"The past is a ghost, the future a dream. All we ever have is Now." —Buddha

Worrier or Warrior?

Which one are you? Your answer to that question makes such a huge difference in finding your abundant life.

A worrier is someone who constantly frets about the past and fears the future. A worrier is so enmeshed in thinking thoughts of other times or problems or grocery lists or worries that he or she completely misses out on the present moment. A worrier trades the magically mundane of the present moment (sunlight filtering through the blinds, children's giggles) for phantom problems that exist only in his or her mind. Unless it is happening right *now*, it can't be acted upon or affected. If it isn't something we can defeat or change right this moment, it only steals our time and energy and options.

"Now Warriors," on the other hand, are constantly aware of the present moment. Their very survival depends on it. They need to know where they are at all times, what is in their immediate environment, what is available as a tool, and what action needs to be taken to achieve their results. They can respond to any situation that arises because they are focused on what is happening right then. They are not burdened by past regrets or fears of tomorrow; they will address tomorrow when it comes. They are doing whatever they can in the present, knowing that is how they will weave it into a future they desire. But they can only act in the now.

Being in the moment is one of the most important habits that must be cultivated.

"You can always cope with the now, but you can never cope with the future, nor do you have to," wrote Eckhart Tolle in *The Power of Now*. You never cope with the future because it must become the present before you can react to it. Rarely does anything bad happen in the now, but when it does and if it does, you are present. You can choose how to respond. You are a warrior.

The majority of each day is not spent living in the present moment but sitting catatonic in front of a mechanical device or imagining negative scenarios in the future. What if... "I lose my job, the stock market crashes, I never get married, I can't pay the bills, I can't get ahead, I'm too old to do it". You know the list.

You may be feeling sorry for yourself regarding what happened in the past. "Why did that have to happen? Why didn't I do that then?" You may have a reason for not being happy, and you continue to nurse this feeling for a long, long time.

You have no control over the past or the future, only over the now. And the future never gets here—it becomes the now.

Think of the things you have feared that might happen in the future. Now think of your everyday life. Did any of those horrific things happen? The answer is probably no, at least to the extent you worried. For those things that did happen, did worrying change or help anything?

Unless you chose to take action based on your worries—something you can only do (make a choice) in the present moment—the answer again is no. And you have then wasted many present moments worrying about the future.

Don't be a worrier, be a warrior.

Stay aware of each moment. See the trees swaying, smell the rain, and hear the bees. Respond to your kids; pat the dog. Visualize and daydream with positive purpose. We live our lives on autopilot, letting our days pass us by, surrounding ourselves by a catatonic fog of helplessness.

This choice to make friends with the present moment is extremely important on our abundance journey. Once you identify your abundance goal and start paying attention to it, the Universe conspires in your favor. But if you aren't paying attention, if you've check out of the now, you will miss the opportunities, the serendipities, and the coincidences that the Universe is sending to show you the way to your dreams. Be a warrior.

"Life happens when you are busy making other plans."

—John Lennon

From my journal:

"I was visiting my grandsons this weekend when I unexpectedly became ill in the middle of the night. My morning ritual with my oldest, Henry, is to get up as soon as I hear his little feet on the floor. We get to spend the morning together before the others wake up.

"That morning I stayed in bed, but when I opened my eyes, there was little Henry, eye level, inches from my face, smiling at me with Curious George in one hand and his coveted blanket in his other.

"'Grandma, let's play.'

"I've never been sick at his house before, and when I told him, he said, 'That's okay, I'll stay here and play.' He crawled into bed, as my head and stomach were churning, and started playing on my iPad. (I'm never really sure which one he likes more, me or the iPad.)

"After a while he informed me he'd be right back; he knew what would make me feel better. Back in he trotted with the cardboard lid to a game box (just the lid), and in it were objects he wanted to share: two dinosaur pieces, so we would each have a dinosaur to play with; four 'matching' cards from the Match the Card game, none of them matching; one plastic credit card from his play cash register; and various other treasures that he had gathered up, found a box in which to carry them, and brought to me so we could play.

"The gesture melted my heart. He wanted to be near me, to play his made-up game of fighting dinosaurs that needed a credit card for some reason. He brought what he could carry, he used natural resources he found to transport them, he invented things we could do lying down, and he was happy to share.

"He didn't worry if he had brought the right thing, if it was enough, or what others would say. He made do with what he had and offered it joyfully. What a lesson we could all learn!

"To assess a situation, decide how to make it better; use resources at your disposal; use your imagination to implement them, knowing it's enough; and joyfully share. I am so blessed for card-carrying dinosaurs and for my family."

But how do we do that? How do we become warriors of the now? Awareness, once again, is the key.

As many times a day as you can, remember to do the following:

Wear a bracelet that says "now."

Write the word on your palm (that was my palm pilot).

Leave cards with the word *now* printed on them in plain view on your mirror, car radio, ceiling, cabinets, etc.

Set your smartphone to go off at certain intervals.

Pick out an object that reminds you to stay in the now.

And then, when you are present:

Take a long breath and become a warrior.

Look at your surroundings, the clouds, the people, your hands.

Listen to the sounds of the city, or thunder, or the wind in the trees.

Feel the hard desk or soft cotton.

Anything to anchor your thoughts in the present moment.

The more you do this, the more you will want to do this. The split-second respite from worry or fear that staying in the present moment brings feels like a cool breeze of calm—an interlude from the self- imposed prison of a worrier.

"Unease, anxiety, tension, stress, worry—all forms of fear— are caused by too much future, and not enough presence."

—Eckhart Tolle

Remind yourself many times a day to appreciate that exact moment. If you are driving, drive. Feel the steering wheel, pay attention to the traffic, listen to music and really hear it. When you're taking a shower, pause and feel the warm water washing over your body. When you're eating, feel the texture and temperature of the food, taste the flavors. Pay attention to life; you are a warrior now.

Time is the one commodity we cannot replace. Please don't squander it. We are on preprogrammed autopilot for so much of our lives. The more moments we can reclaim from this malady—the more moments we claim for joy and for action, and for appreciating surprise serendipities—and the more we actually feel alive.

Put down the smartphone and slowly back away. I mean it. We use it to anesthetize our brains. We use it to look at stupid cat pictures (not that cats are stupid), say snotty things about people we don't know, play solitaire, and post stupid cat pictures (see above). We waste precious time. It's a habit, it's comfortable, and it fritters away the most precious moment of now.

Be a now warrior. Turn off the computer and the TV, and see what is in front of you. We have become afraid of our thoughts or lack of them, afraid of silence, and afraid of truly engaging in life. Play with your kids, look them in the eyes, teach them to cook. Go on a walk, write an old friend (using stamps and everything), or write in your journal.

Just be quiet and let the silence wash over you. Do whatever you need to do to be vigilant and remain focused on the present moment. You are a warrior; your very life and your awareness of your existence depend on it.

Learn to Quiet Your Mind

Because you are a now warrior, there is another essential tool that helps you reclaim your ability to stay in the now and live an abundant life. You must learn to quiet your mind.

There are so many outside influences: noise, sights, opinions, options, channels, websites—all a cacophony of useless information that our five senses can access. We need to take control over what we choose to allow into our mind (remember you can only choose in the present moment).

We need to constantly be *aware* (there's that word again) of our abundance goal and flood our mind with only positive options regarding that goal. For instance, watch documentaries on the subject, read about it, take language lessons, or listen to beautiful music. Choose the information you allow in. Feed the good wolf.

In addition to choosing the environment we want to be exposed to, we also need to become comfortable with silence. We need to learn how to eliminate the outside noise and focus on one thing—or "no thing." We need to silence our mind. The more we silence our mind, the more control we have over our ability to live in the now.

The Monkey Mind

A term coined by the Buddha, the monkey mind is when your mind is going one hundred miles an hour in all directions. Your train of thought is so out of control that you completely forget where you boarded. And regrettably, that is usually the mode of transportation our mind reverts to.

You know, "Got to remember to get milk ... is dairy good or

bad for us this month ... I forgot my yoga pants ... they are in the dirty clothes ... I forgot to do the laundry ... oh no, Johnny doesn't have clean underwear ... my mother said to always wear clean underwear in case you are in a wreck ... oh no, what if Johnny gets in a wreck ... squirrel ..."

We need to learn to train that monkey to serve us, not lead us down the path of unfocused dribble.

How to do that? By learning to quiet your mind through the practice of meditation. Although it has a bad rep of having to sit cross-legged on a hard floor for hours in silence, meditation is much kinder in reality.

It can be as simple and short as one deep breath in and out with a quiet mind. Just stay with it, think of your breath—and only your breath—and nothing else. Tell your monkey mind to take a short nap!

Exercises

1. Put down this book and look around you. Take in a deep breath. Slowly let it out. As you do this, concentrate on everything you see in your area. Be as specific as possible.
2. Take in another breath, and feel all the different textures in your space. Slowly let it out. Make a mental note of how they feel: soft pillow, hard glass, hot coffee, scratchy chair ...
3. Again breathe in and out, and smell whatever is in your vicinity. Go outside if possible. Smell the wind and the grass. Go to the kitchen and smell spices. Smell the cookies baking. Pay attention to the smells.
4. Be quiet. Take a breath; let it out. What do you hear? What noises have always been present that you have ignored?
5. Get a piece of fruit and admire its beauty. Then slowly eat it, noticing the taste, the texture, and the smell.

Repeat every day!

Chapter 7

Quieting the Mind

"You can't make peace in the outer world until we make peace with ourselves." —Dalai Lama

"The aim of life is to live, and to live means to be aware, joyously, drunkenly, serenely, divinely aware." —Henry Miller

"There is more to life than increasing the speed."
—Mahatma Gandhi

"The goal of meditation is not to control your thoughts; it is to stop letting them control you." —Unknown

Back in the day, when I wasn't so enlightened—before my heart said, "Stop this madness"—I used to start my day, before going to court, by taking what I referenced as my "wonder walk." My intention was to take thirty minutes and stroll through my beautiful neighborhood, admiring the big trees, walking paths, lakes, and even a waterfall—just enjoying nature.

I wouldn't walk half a block from the house before my monkey mind jumped on board and had a party.

"Um, what do I have at court today? ... Okay, I have the Smith case (the names have been changed to protect the guilty). This is what I will argue ... Oh, that sounds good. Okay, what

will the other side argue, just so I know how I will respond? ...
Well, that pisses me off ... Okay, so this is how I will respond ..."
I played the entire argument in my mind. "Hey, Mrs. Smith owes
me money; I need to get it from her ... she is always behind ...
My account receivables are down this month ... Damn, I forgot
about that bill ..."

I'd worry about my kids; I'd worry about the environment;
I'd worry about politics; I'd worry if I had enough food in case
of the apocalypse. By the time I returned home, two things had
happened. I hadn't enjoyed nature one iota (the present moment),
and I was upset. (My husband dubbed it my worry walk.)

This went on for years until I learned to put a quiet space, a
silence, in my life.

We must become aware of a space in our lives, a space most of
us don't even know exists—not in geography, not in the physical,
but inside of ourselves. We must learn to pry open this space to
let a light shine in: the light of the infinite.

But space scares us. We hurry from one task to another as not
to waste time in this space. If we find there is a lag between two
chores, appointments, or TV shows, we grab our smartphones
to fill the void with Facebook gossip or games of solitaire. We fill
a space in a conversation with idle babble. We fill our lives with
unnecessary clutter because buying things keeps us from this
space. Moving and cleaning the clutter keeps us from this space.
Placing value on accumulations keeps us from this space. We do
anything we can to keep ourselves busy: mindless TV, constant
web surfing, endless and/or uncomfortable chatter, anything to
keep us from entering this space.

We are afraid of this space—the space of quiet, inactive "non-
thought." We are afraid to sit quietly with ourselves and discover
no one is home.

If you don't believe me, stop right now and set the timer on
your phone for one minute, just one minute. (And yes, I know
the phone is only inches from your hand in case there might be a

nanosecond available to glance at stupid cat pictures. Once again, it's the pictures, not the cats, that are stupid.)

Now start the timer, close your eyes, and just sit. Empty your mind of everything and just sit quietly with yourself. Go!

Okay, come back. Unless you are a seasoned meditator, your process probably went something like this:

> I can do this, piece of cake, no-brainer.
> Hey, no-brainer, it's supposed to be a no-brainer.
> Okay. (Blank mind for two seconds.)
> Wait, what does that look like?
> No thoughts, okay, think of no thoughts.
> (Blank mind for five seconds.)
> I have an itch.
> Damn, I forgot to email Frank.
> I'll do it when I get done.
> How much longer? I'll just glance at the timer.
> Damn again, it's only been fourteen seconds.
> Okay, I can do this (squint eyes, grit teeth).
> (Five more seconds go by.)
> Well, this is just stupid. I have so much to do, I forgot …!
> (Squirm in your chair.)
> (Start a mental to-do list.)
> (Grab a pen and actually write a to-do list so you won't forget.)

Am I correct? We are conditioned for constant thinking. We must keep our brain busy. Or our brain keeps us busy. It is like the runaway train with no one at the wheel. It's continual, it's incessant, and it's exhausting.

It's time we learned how to slow it down, stop it, and perhaps choose a new destination.

We must master this concept to be able to use the six intellectual facilities we have talked about—to choose new thoughts that will automatically induce different emotions (vibrations) that cause a different response, which produces a different response from the Universe.

We must learn to quiet our mind and be comfortable in this quietness in order to allow a space between outside stimuli and a reasoned, inspired, or intuitive thought to emerge. We then can choose a response based on our authentic self, on our own amazing goals, and on our genuine abundance.

According to Eckhart Tolle in *The Power of Now*, "Spaces are so important in our lives. Without a space between letters, there would be no words. Without a space between notes, there would be no music. Without a space between thoughts, there would be no consciousness. Without a space between an action and a response, there can be no responsibility."

Without a space between breaths, there can be no silence. Without silence, we cannot connect to the divine.

"Silent and listen use the same, exact letters. Think about it."

—Unknown

A Zen proverb recommends, "You should meditate for twenty minutes each day unless you're too busy. Then you should meditate for an hour."

"If you think you're too busy to take twenty minutes a day to meditate, you don't understand what meditation can do for you," writes Emma Seppala of Stanford University *(20 Scientific Reasons to Start Meditating Today, Psychology Today,* September 2013).

To paraphrase that article, (I've added some additional reasons that were listed as subheads) here are some reasons to start meditation:

1. Decreases pain
2. Decreases inflammation at the cellular level
3. Boosts your happiness
4. Increases positive emotion

5. Decreases depression
6. Decreases anxiety
7. Decreases stress
8. Boosts your social life
9. Increases social connection and emotional intelligence
10. Makes you more compassionate
11. Makes you feel less lonely
12. Boosts your self-control
13. Improves your ability to regulate your emotions
14. Improves your ability to introspect
15. Changes your brain (for the better)
16. Increases gray matter
17. Increases volume in areas related to emotion regulation, positive emotions, and self-control
18. Increases cortical thickness in areas related to paying attention
19. Improves your productivity (yup, by doing nothing)
20. Increases your focus and attention
21. Improves your ability to multitask
22. Improves your memory
23. Improves your ability to be creative and think outside the box
24. Makes you wise(r).

Many more peer-reviewed articles confirm the amazing benefits of meditating even twenty minutes a day. I hope this convinces you of its necessity in your life.

There are many great, simple books that can get you started. (Some are listed on my website in my book list under Resources.) However, for those of you who won't find the time because you are too darn busy to go to amazon.com and buy one, here is a very easy, gentle overview of how to get started.

What you need is you. That's it. Just you. And you always have you with you, so it's a no-brainer (which it literally is) to be able to meditate anywhere.

To start a routine first thing in the morning, find a quiet spot and sit in a comfortable chair (no need to sit cross-legged on the floor). Sitting straight up will help your breathing and keep you awake.

Set a timer. Start slow, five minutes at first. Soft, low music is comforting. A scented candle is nice. Close your eyes; quiet your mind.

Breathe in slowly, breathe out slowly, and stay still for a moment. Keep your attention on your breath. If a thought comes in, which it always will, imagine it's a cloud and let it lovingly float away. One breath with a quiet mind is a meditation. Do it again. Do it whenever you have a minute; do it right before you go off to battle in the boardroom. But do it.

The first time I attempted to meditate, I envisioned a radar screen, the kind they use in an airport control tower. I visualized the hand sweeping around my head, starting at my forehead and moving continuously clockwise. Everywhere it touched, the hand would quiet that portion of the brain—that chatter we don't even know is constantly taking place—until it returned to the forehead. For the first time in memory, my mind was still. Calm.

Another breath in, another sweep of the dial, a breath out, and silence. I'm sure I wasn't involved in this sequence for very long, but for the rest of the day, I literally was euphoric—enough of a difference that I had to ask myself if I had taken drugs. Ah yes, the drug of silence.

Another excerpt from my journal:

"I quit arguing with my ego to be quiet in meditation. I quit trying to stay focused (unfocused?) and fighting between thoughts. My sweet precious ego was just trying to get my attention, and my soul just wanted to rest. But it was a fist-clenched kind of dance. I'd try very hard to stay "non" (calm, clear, silent), but the mundane thoughts of everyday slipped in. It's many moments before I realize I am not non anymore. So I metaphorically grab my arm and pull me back to the non, still clenching my ego with one hand to keep it in place. It's like meditating while holding the hand of a two-year-old. When I was more ego than non, I would judge myself and feel bad. Who is keeping score? It's me versus me? When I learn to relax, step back, love my little ego, and say, "We're resting now"—when I get closer to my higher self and farther from that ego that throws temper tantrums demanding that we are needed in the real world—I am connected to divinity.

"And my poor body is the battleground along for the ride (well, it actually is the ride). When I am more in my higher self, I want to take care of it as a beloved child. On the other hand, when I am more in ego, I boss it around, insult it, demand it stay up longer, work harder, and eat less.

Meditating can be a metaphor for using my higher self in everyday life to appreciate in silence this amazing vehicle (my body) that I have been given in this life.

For the purpose of discussing meditation, there are three parts of our consciousness: the ego, the soul, and the higher self.

The ego is our personality that has been programmed and constructed over this lifetime, our commander in chief.

Our soul is our consciousness. It is eternal, aware of what the other self, the ego, is doing. It can view from a distance with a perspective the ego lacks.

"What a liberation to realize that the 'voice in my head' is not who I am. Who am I then? That one who sees that."

—Eckhart Tolle

Every wonder who you are talking to when you talk to yourself? You inherently know there are two parts of you, the one doing the doing, and the one that is aware you are doing it.

"What is a conscience? I'll tell ya! A conscience is that still small voice people won't listen to. That's just the trouble with the world today." —Jiminy Cricket

The third part of the amazing you is the higher self, which our soul connects to, the divinity of life.

It is a continuous spectrum, from the ego that blends into consciousness (soul) that transcends into the higher self that connects to the infinite. They melt together, always one. But in this lifetime, they can be imagined as separate, sometimes even nonexistent.

Our goal is to quiet that yappy commander in chief, who is used to always being in control (ego), and allow our consciousness (soul) a little glimmer of light, a crack in the armor, an instant to connect us to our higher self.

This is not unlike a seed planted in the ground. The outside shell must crack open to allow the growth from the inside to peek through. This is the same with our ego self. We think it protects us from the harsh realities of the outside, but what it really does is stop the amazing, miraculous growth from inside of us to appear.

We must allow a crack, a silence, a breath, a non-moment to appear in our busy, ego-controlled lives and allow the consciousness (the soul) to whisper, "Remember me; I've always been here and always will be. Rest awhile. Let's talk. I've missed you. You can trust me. I am you; you are me. We are one; we are divine. The answers are here. More importantly, so are the questions."

And then you take another breath. I find that the space between the breathing—when you are not in or out, just still and being—is the sweet spot. This is where the door is open. This is where the connection to the infinite resides. And then we breathe again.

I had an experience shortly after I began a quasi-regular meditation practice. I was opening a door (normal door, normal day); however, when I pushed it open, for a split second I was opening the door into another dimension. I felt, saw, met, and was engulfed by a wave of love, and different personalities surrounded me. I felt as if I had opened a door to heaven, and the angels were just as surprised as I was. I said or thought or exclaimed, "Oh, it's you," as if I had come home and been reunited with everyone I had loved. I knew them and somehow remembered them. I felt such unconditional love that it took my breath away. And then the metaphorical door closed, and I was outside again. This all happened in an instant, but somehow I knew they were still there—still and always.

I had cracked open that shell and saw a glimmer of eternity. I knew in some way it was associated with my meditation practice and the ability to access some inner part of me.

A meditation practice is so important and so easy. You just sit with yourself, be yourself, be quiet, be silent, and be open.

"I think ninety-nine times and find nothing. I stop thinking, swim in silence, and the truth comes to me," Albert Einstein said.

When you silence your mind, you can tap into an energy field, referred to by many different names over the millennia: the field of potentiality, the unified field, the zero point field, the Hindu Akashic record, the Source, God.

This sea of energy permeates, penetrates, and fills the inner spaces of the universe. It is a quivering, invisible source of energy that has recently been detected and acknowledged by science (although the interpretation of this field is still hotly debated).

The ancients referred to this field as the energy that unites us all. It contains all the information, all the communication, and all the knowledge in the universe.

And the ancient masters tell us that when you tap into it, all knowledge of the ages is at your command. (More about this is the science chapter.)

Many individuals have reported blending with this field through meditation. These individuals (Einstein, Edison, Tesla, and Steve Jobs, just to name a few) discovered, invented, and recognized amazing concepts that propelled our society to the next level. They credited their new ideas to this one thing: they quieted their minds, went into a different level of consciousness (trance), and received information from outside of themselves.

Steve Jobs reported that during a Zen mindfulness meditation, he literally saw the smartphone in his mind. He went on to say, "When it {mind} calms, there's room to hear more subtle things—that's when your intuition starts to blossom and you start to see things more clearly and be in the present more. Your mind just slows down, and you see a tremendous expanse in that moment. You see so much more than you could see before."

We can all do this. In the chapter on abundance, I'm sure some of you skeptics murmured, "Yeah, right, she's crazy. There is only so much to go around. There is a scarcity of things."

We need to become aware that the field contains abundance, and this abundance is our birthright, attainable and accessible. When we tap into this field, this level of consciousness through meditation, we can lower our shields, stop resisting, and silence our preprogrammed conditioning. When we just listen, new ideas, new paths, new inventions, and new dreams will come to us. This is our pathway to our genuine abundance in all things, for everyone. This is our path to our worthy ideal.

"Praying is talking to the Universe. Meditation is listening to it." —Unknown

We learn to create more abundance and not compete for what we think is a limited supply. God, the Creator, created us in his own image. And what was God's image? A creator. He created us to be creators—not competitors fighting over scraps. We all create when we tap into this field and dream new ways to produce, write, invent, and build.

Life is always expanding and creating. God is always expanding and creating. A tree is always expanding, creating leaves and incalculable seeds for future forests, which in turn, do the same. New stars are formed, new kittens are born, and new grass is grown. There is no struggle. Grass doesn't struggle to grow. Neither should we.

When you learn to quiet your mind and attach to your higher self, which melts into the field, you attach to all creation and begin to create. New ideas come to and through you. More love comes to and through you. New ways of doing things appear. You are introduced to something unknown until then. You don't have to struggle to grow. You never had to.

We don't have to compete for enough horses for transportation; we created cars. We don't have to compete for enough wood for fires; we discovered how to harness infinite electricity. We won't have to compete for oil; we'll tap into the wind and the sun and ultimately the field. When there is a need, someone will be inspired to create a new solution, not compete over existing answers.

"We cannot solve problems with the same thinking we used to create them." — Albert Einstein

"And in our own lives, when we silence our mind and listen, divinity speaks." —Me

"Meditation is a gift you give yourself to find yourself." —Me

"You had the answer all along, my dear."
—Glenda the Good Witch

Chapter 8

Gratitude Is the Attitude

"The ultimate source of happiness is a mental decision."
—Buddha

"Each day comes bearing gifts. Untie the ribbon."
—Unknown

Happiness is an inside job. It is a choice in each moment. It is a choice to think a different thought or choose a new perspective for a situation. It is not always easy. It is always worth it.

Note from the Author:
Choosing happiness is not always easy. During a difficult time in our marriage, my husband had an affair, which produced a baby. There were, of course, a myriad of ways to respond to this. The immediate reaction was to divorce. But being a divorce attorney, I knew it causes different problems, problems that could be worse.

I took a big breath and a step back. We went to counseling, decided to stay together, and viewed the baby as a blessing, an addition of love to our lives.

There were many blessings revealed: Baby Austin, of course; the fact Austin's mother was kind and a great mom; the discovery we were all able to work together, united by a common love; and the opportunity to grow from that experience.

I learned to ignore snotty comments and judgmental glances from unkind people. I appreciated my life and all the people in it. The blessings continue to this day. I chose to use my facility of perception and viewed the situation differently. I used my facility of will to get through difficult times and my imagination to create a wonderful future. I chose happiness, and it has been returned to me tenfold.

What you sow, so shall you reap.

In our discussion of the paradigm shift, we discovered we can choose to reprogram an outdated, involuntary system of unconsciously coasting through life.

In the chapter on our six intellectual faculties, we discovered we can choose to respond using these faculties, instead of reacting with our preprogrammed five senses.

We learned how to quiet our mind and provide a space in our daily moments to choose a new way to respond and reclaim our response-ability and, therefore, our destiny.

When we keep our ultimate dreams in the back of our consciousness, a roadmap will be provided for the choices we can make. When we internalize our new goals with constant, spaced repetition and with emotion, we can change our internal program.

When we allow a space to open, we can see new options, perspectives, and insights that serve us in a better way. The universe echoes our new response with the same energy we put out: positive energy-positive response-positive universal reaction (see chapter 11).

Our attitude is comprised of three parts: our thoughts, our actions, and our feelings. When they are in harmony, it is very powerful.

"Happiness is harmony between a man and the life that he leads." —Albert Camus

The old saying "Her heart wasn't in it" is a perfect example of not being in harmony. When we feel pressured to do something out of fear, guilt, or weakness—while in our heart, our soul, we don't want to do it—the low energy we expend and our lukewarm actions reflect a lackluster attempt on our part. If you do this too often you will lose a part of yourself.

We must be aware of the three parts of attitude when we are discussing gratitude, the ultimate attitude.

Let's talk about gratitude. It is the highest frequency in which you can physically vibrate. You can choose to be grateful for many things—counting the blessings you already have, appreciating the opportunities you know are coming, and being grateful for the path that led you here. There is always something to be grateful for. If initially you can't find something, look a little deeper, try another memory, use your imagination, listen to your breath, hear the silence, or feel the sun.

"I would maintain that thanks are the highest form of thought and that gratitude is happiness doubled by wonder."

—G. K. Chesterton

There have been exciting new studies in psychology about the positive effects that gratitude/happiness (you can't have one without the other) have on our physical body, on our workplace productivity, and on our ability to be more creative. But for the sake of our purpose here, there are two points I'd like to make.

1. It is always your decision to choose gratitude.
2. When you perceive that you are in a situation in which gratitude would not be authentic or harmonious with reality, stop, be silent, listen, and remember.

Remember times in your past when something bad happened (or at the time you recognized it as negative). Now take that timeline forward to something good that happened. You will realize that the good thing couldn't have happened unless the negative thing had been experienced in the past. (Good and bad are judgment calls; once you get enough perspective or distance, there is no judgment, only understanding.)

When you do this exercise, you will see a serendipitous path that unfolds, leading you to something positive. You will then become grateful for the negative thing, at least for the purpose of the good thing happening.

When I review my own life, one specific incident stands out: the night I began to have anxiety attacks. They were the scariest, most uncontrollable moments I can remember. Not knowing when they would appear and not having any way to escape from them, they controlled my day-to-day activities. I was afraid to go places, to get on an airplane, and to go to court. But without the intense nudge from my higher self, I wouldn't have followed this path. I wouldn't have found answers to questions I couldn't even articulate back then. I wouldn't be here today, sharing with you. I am now so grateful for that set of circumstances that led me to this information and transformation.

"Acknowledging the good that you already have in your life is the foundation for all abundance." —Eckhart Tolle

View your current circumstances with a new perspective, one that trusts the Universe to turn them into something positive. Appreciate the connection to something better in the future. This part of your story may not yet be finished. You may still be in the middle of this particular adventure. Have faith that the end of the story will enable you to understand why you had to go through these seemingly difficult circumstances. If it's not a happy ending, it's not the end.

Do this exercise by choosing to look at the good things in your present life. Go backward until you realize that an unfavorable situation had to occur to lead you to this present time, and recognize the good that came out of something negative. It is essential to choose gratitude. It is your connection to divinity. It is your roadmap out of despair.

"Do not be anxious about anything, but in every situation, by prayer and petition, with thanksgiving, present your requests to God and the peace of God, which transcends all understanding, will guard your heart and mind." —Philippians 4: 6–7

Try to perceive that your life evolves into good things, using past circumstances. Have faith that this difficulty will also evolve into a positive outcome. If you are having trouble seeing anything positive coming from where you are now, remember that you may be in the middle of the story and imagine a positive outcome.

Jesus said to be thankful unto the Lord. Not that the Big Guy needed it, but this gratitude, this highest vibration, connects you to the unified field, divinity, the Source, the Universe.

Jesus (as well as all other masters of love) gave us the key to peaceful minds and hearts. It is for *our* benefit to choose gratitude, as it enables us to plug into infinite knowledge, clarity, creativity, and love.

American psychologist William James once said, "When you have to make a choice and you don't make it, that, itself is a choice."

Make the choice to be thankful. When you are grateful, you exude that energy, and the Universe returns even more to you to be grateful for.

"Fear not, it is your father's good pleasure to give you the Kingdom." —Luke 12:32

He, it, they, the Universe wants you to have it all, to have genuine abundance. It is your birthright, your inheritance. But the only way you can have it all is to be in the receiving mode. And the only way to be in the receiving mode is to be on the frequency that allows you to receive more. Choose the gratitude frequency. The gratitude frequency is where the magic begins to happen. It is because you are grateful that more is given.

If you gave a person a gift and he or she was not thankful, would you be inclined to give that person more gifts? What if people were extremely appreciative and thankful for whatever small token they received? Which action on their part would encourage more giving on your part? This is the same with the Universe. If you are grateful for what you have, the gratitude frequency attracts to you more things to be grateful for.

"Gratitude is a currency that we can mint for ourselves and spend without fear of bankruptcy."

— Fred De Witt Van Amburgh

Giving and receiving is the same gesture: hands outstretched, palms open. You can't give or receive with clenched fists. When you are grateful, you realize there is abundance. When you realize there is abundance, you want to share. You stretch your palms and arms out to others with treasures. When your arms are outstretched, you can receive gifts in return.

It is a magical, universal dance. Being grateful attaches you to the Source. What you put out, you receive in return. (Each action creates an equal and opposite reaction.) When you are grateful, you willingly give. When you give willingly, you should receive graciously.

Do not stop this mystical flow by refusing to give from your abundance. Do not stop this magical flow by refusing to receive from others' abundance (a compliment, a helping hand, an unexpected gift).

Begin from wherever you are right now. You have an

abundance of smiles, hugs, love, and hope. Give abundance away. It spirals up to bigger and bigger gifts.

Never think you have nothing to give. When you become *aware* of the power that flows to and through you and your connection to the divine, you can quiet your mind, ask for direction, and give what you have in your current situation. Remember, there are always credit card-carrying dinosaurs somewhere in your life.

"Give, and it will be given to you. They will pour into your lap a good measure, pressed down, shaken together, running over. For by your standard of measure it will be measured to you in return." —Luke 6:38

When we reclaim our power of being grateful and realize we do have something of value to offer, we stop being victims. We become generous benefactors. We continue to give more, get more, and appreciate more until it becomes a continuous motion of life.

"Be thankful for what you have; you'll end up having more. If you concentrate on what you don't have, you will never, ever have enough." —Oprah Winfrey

"It is not happy people who are thankful. It is thankful people who are happy." —Unknown

"The law of attraction brings you more of what you put your attention on. It's a no-brainer, people. Choose gratitude." —Me

"When I started counting my blessings, my whole life turned around." —Willie Nelson

Exercise

Start a gratitude journal. Every day write down five things you are grateful for. Write in cursive, write at the same time each day, and write in the same book. Write something different for each entry. It's amazing how creative you can get when you must think of new things to be grateful for. You begin to look all day long for things to write in your journal. And guess what? You start seeing more and more things to be grateful for.

Chapter 9

A Spirit Being Human

"We are not human beings having a spiritual experience, we are spirits having a human experience."
—Pierre Teilhard de Chardin

"This isn't my first rodeo". —Me

"Have you ever wondered where you were before "you were"? Where your beloved children were before they were in your arms?"

"Before I formed you in your mother's womb, I knew you."
—Jeremiah 1:5

As we begin to go down this rabbit hole of spirituality and eternal life, it might be helpful to first examine some additional information and employ some logical thinking.

Statistics tell us that 95 percent of all the people in the world believe in a higher power. Aldous Huxley, a twentieth-century author, coined the phrase "the perennial philosophy," an idea that all religions can be reduced to three basic concepts: there is a higher power, we are connected to it, and it is eternal. Realizing the high percentage of individuals who believe in a higher power, and understanding the definition of the philosophy behind all the world religions, perhaps we could entertain the following questions:

Do you believe you are more than just a physical body?

Do you believe you have a soul or a spirit?

Do you believe that when you die, there is an afterlife?

Do you believe that this afterlife is eternal?

Do you believe that the Higher Source is eternal?

Do you believe that *eternal* means there is no beginning or no ending?

Do you believe, as science tells us, that energy can be neither created nor destroyed, it just changes form?

Do you believe your spirit is eternal?

Can you believe that your eternal spirit did not just begin with this one lifetime?

Can you entertain the thought that perhaps you existed as a spiritual being before this lifetime?

Since energy can be neither created nor destroyed, do you see that if your spirit is energy, it can be neither created nor destroyed?

Can you believe that perhaps your spirit is divine energy, connected to a Divine Source, which has no beginning and no ending?

Keeping an open mind, understanding this may be new material to some, let's continue. You may not believe that you existed in a different body in a prior lifetime, but try to see if you could fathom your spirit existing before this lifetime.

I still have a vivid and remarkable memory of being very young, still in a crib, in a bedroom with cowboy and Indian wallpaper, in a house from which we moved before I was three. I put my hand in front of my face and formed a thought, a concept: I am conscious, again.

Although I was a precocious child, I am sure the word *conscious* was not in my vocabulary. And the memory is a mature, old soul memory, not like the others I can recall of playing with my sisters and chasing the cat.

It has remained an anchor and a beacon at different stages of my life. It provided both stability and a promise of a bigger—and I mean bigger—existence.

I was in first grade when I realized, after the first week of all-day school, that this school thing wasn't just a passing fancy of my mother. I was expected to go every single day for the next twelve years (turned out it was nineteen). I remember lying in bed when a mature thought bubbled up. "Not again, I already know all this stuff. I can't take it again ..." This wasn't from a perspective of a six-year-old throwing a temper tantrum but from the perspective of, well, an old spirit back for more adventure.

These kinds of thoughts would come and go throughout my younger days. Most of the time I was mentally and emotionally my chronological age, but the old soul "Me" would occasionally pop up its head from playing dodge ball, look around, and register a consciousness far beyond my age.

In grade school, at Christmas, we would draw names to exchange gifts, with a ten-cent limit. (This dates me.) One of the poorest, skinniest girls, who literally wore old, tattered clothes, drew my name. When we unwrapped our presents, I had a six-inch, purple velveteen hair bow as my present. Other kids twittered a little, as they were holding yo-yos or a set of jacks. My first thought was *What am I, with short hair, going to do with this ugly bow?*

Above, outside, and deep inside the third grade Me, that spirit Me picked me up, took me over, hugged her, and told her I loved it. What did she have to sacrifice to give me this Christmas gift that rivaled the wise men? There was deep empathy, compassion, and unconditional love emanating from me. I remember it as an adult would remember something, not as I remember my other childhood events.

At fifteen, I was bored living in my small Midwestern town and sitting on the trunk of our family's only vehicle, a beat-up

Ford Falcon. I was lamenting about my limited options of what I could do without a driver's license when that old Me once again appeared in my teenage consciousness.

"What a waste to just sit here. When Edison was this age, he was inventing the future. There is so much you came here to do. You had such optimistic plans for this time around. Get off the darn car and do something, read something, learn something."

It was outside of me, yet Me. I thought how deep and insightful I was, yet somehow I knew it was a deeper, older Me communicating with the fifteen-year-old wearing cat-eyed, rhinestone glasses.

As a junior in college, I was walking across the campus, hating my current major, when a clear message came to me. "You were supposed to go to law school, stupid!" It had never even entered my mind until that second. (I have been a practicing attorney for the last thirty-seven years. It has served me, and hopefully my clients, well.)

Consciousness. Again. Knowing I had to go through school, again.

Feeling a universal love toward a fellow human being. Knowing I had been here before. Knowing I had a bigger plan this time. Knowing there was an intent for this time.

Have you ever felt like that—beyond intuition, beyond logic, beyond time? The awareness of a continuing, infinite Me?

There have been many documented studies performed by credible medical doctors, psychiatrists, and scientists that point to a consciousness outside of the physical body that survives death.

Michael Newton, a PhD in counseling psychology and a certified master hypnotherapist, has written numerous books regarding the information he received from people under hypnosis, a state in which they are incapable of lying. In *Journey of the Souls (Llewellyn Worldwide, LTD., 2002)*, he compiled the stories of all the individuals, none of them knowing the others, and found remarkable, almost identical experiences reported of life before life and other lifetimes lived. When people reported prior lifetimes and specific information from those lifetimes, research was conducted to verify the facts presented under hypnosis. Almost universally the facts about the prior life were true, something the hypnotized person had no way of ascertaining.

The Bible speaks about reincarnation. In Mark 11:11–15, Jesus states that John the Baptist was the reincarnation of the prophet Elias: "Among them that are born of women there hath not risen a greater than John the Baptist ... And if ye will receive it, this is Elias."

Many of the early church fathers believed and wrote, "The idea that the soul existed before the body and is fundamental to the concept of reincarnation ..." (Origen, AD 185–254). Saint Gregory, Saint Augustine, Saint Ambrose, Pope Gregory I, and Saint Basil are additional church fathers who believed in a life before this birth and a life after this death.

Whether you have never thought about this idea or have rejected it outright, perhaps you could look at this information with a different perspective and see if anything touches your soul.

Bear with me for a moment as we jump to another topic, free will, and how it can shed some light on these questions.

God gave us the opportunity to make choices in this lifetime, and there is an inherent perception of free will in all religions. The Bible also states, "Now the Lord is the Spirit and where the Spirit of the Lord is, there is freedom" (2 Corinthians 3:17).

What if freedom—defined as self-determination, autonomy, choice, free will—didn't just start in this lifetime, in the limited environment that we find ourselves, in a limited culture, after an arbitrary age?

What if free will belongs to the spirit Me, always has and always will?

"What if we didn't just get pushed off a cloud or drew the short straw?" asks author Mike Dooley.

What if we bravely chose the life we now have? What if this

time around we wanted to feel, explore, or experience something our other lifetimes hadn't offered?

How could the small, starving child in India ever have free will? What choices are there in misery? But what if, just for a second, you consider that free will happens prior to this lifetime, that we all get to exercise free will from a perspective that we haven't been able to imagine before? We choose to experience hunger to contrast the opulence in a prior life. We choose to be a victim so someone else can be the victor. We choose to die for a cause so the cause can grow and civilization can evolve.

What if we know it's only temporary like playing a part in a movie? Only we forget it's a movie?

How much more sense would this life make? How much braver would we be, knowing we can lead the charge of Union soldiers into battle, fighting for freedom in one moment and watching reruns of our heroics in heaven the next? Then, after resting awhile, we use our free will to choose a new adventure in time and space and leap again?

Never, ever squandering a life, or a love, or a purpose, or a cause but embracing them all and taking chances.

We would be living life to its fullest instead of tiptoeing around it, trying to escape death. As author Hunter S. Thompson wrote, "Life should not be a journey to the grave with the intention of arriving safely in a pretty, well-preserved body, but rather to skid in broadside in a cloud of smoke, thoroughly used up, totally worn out and loudly proclaiming, 'Wow, what a ride.'"

I stumbled upon, quite by coincidence (wink, wink), a poem called *"The Trial by Existence,"* by Robert Frost. I urge you to print the entire poem from my website and read it from time to time.

I have picked out a few of the stanzas that resonate with our conversation:

Even the bravest that are slain
Shall not dissemble their surprise

On waking to find valor reign,
Even as on earth, in paradise ...
To find that the utmost reward
Of daring should be still to dare."

We bravely, valiantly live a life of heroic measure and live, or
die, for a cause. We know it's temporary. We awaken in heaven,
review our adventure, and then willingly do it again if we choose.
Like a line of brave ten-year-old kids waiting to jump off the high
dive, we realize we still get to dare again.

And from a cliff-top is proclaimed
The gathering of the souls for birth,
The trial by existence named,
The obscuration upon earth.
And the slants spirits trooping by
In stream and cross- and counter-streams
Can but give ear to that sweet cry
For its suggestion of what dreams!

And the more loitering are turned
To view once more the sacrifice
Of those who for some good discerned
Will gladly give up paradise.
And a white shimmering concourse rolls
Toward the throne to witness there
The speeding of devoted souls
Which God make his especial care.

And none are taken but who will,
Having first heard the life read out
That opens earthward, good and ill,
Beyond a shadow of a doubt;
And very beautifully God limns,

And tenderly, life's little dream,
But naught, extenuates or dims,
Setting the thing that is supreme …

The tale of earth's unhonored things
Sound nobler there 'neath the sun;
And the mind whirls and the heart sings,
And a shout greets the daring one.

But always God speaks at the end:
"One thought in agony or strife
The bravest would have by for friend
The memory that he chooses the life;
But the pure fate to which you go
Admits no memory or choice,
Or the woe was not earthly woe
To which you give assenting voice."

And so the choice must be again,
But the last choice is still the same;
And the awe passes wonder then,
And a hush falls for all acclaim.
And God has taken a flower of gold
And broken it, and used therefrom
The mystic link to bend and hold
Spirit to matter till death come.

'Tis the essence of life here,
Though we choose greatly, still to lack
The lasting memory at all clear,
That life has for us on the wrack
Nothing but what we somehow chose …

I envision a gorgeous cliff in heaven, with beautiful, timeless souls gathering to begin a new adventure. They are "sacrificing" paradise for some good "discerned" on earth. These souls, who willingly come to earth, God makes his "especial care."

"None are taken but who will, having first heard the life read out."

We consciously choose a life, a place to be born, our families, circumstances, cultures, trials, and tribulations, as God describes "life's little dream" to each of us. "But naught extenuates or dims, setting the thing that is supreme." You will always know "the thing that is supreme"—your reason for this lifetime—deep in your heart, even if you don't consciously remember anything else. You will know in your soul the reason you jumped off the high dive.

The poet goes on to warn that God tells us the place you go "admits no memory of choice, or … earthly woe to which you give assenting voice." We choose to be here, not remembering our divinity, so we may experience earth in all its splendor, good and bad.

How different would you view your life, and the lives of all people, if that were true? If you knew we all choose this life? Would it answer the question of why some are born in squalor while others in luxury?

Would you perceive others differently? Brave souls returning to conquer an earthly woe? Spirits volunteering to be destitute in the hope of "choosing greatly" and making a difference in the world? Other spirits choosing to see an injustice and right a wrong? Spirits volunteering to provide contrast on this earthly plane so we can experience and decide how we wish to live this life, find our dream, and love our neighbor?

Would it make you more aware that you have inside the "thing that is supreme"? That you were the "daring one" to come here and claim this life and live it to its highest level?

Would it encourage you to be braver, to risk more, or to stand up for worthy causes if you knew it was guaranteed you would ultimately be all right? And then, voluntarily, cut back in line to jump off the high dive for more?

Mike Dooley, one of my faves, wrote this in one of his "Notes from the Universe":

"Every single morning, ever since time began, before the sun even rises, the drums start beating, the choirs start singing, the energy starts rising, and every single soul who has ever lived scurries about the plane of manifestation as a chanting begins … And get louder and louder … And goes faster and faster until … a feverish pitch is reached and the celestial skies part with a clap of thunder, revealing billions upon billions of the most beautiful angels you have ever seen … Every one of them a messenger of hope, and peace, and joy; healers and teachers, comforters and creators. And every one of them about to greet a brand-new day in time and space with a morning yawn, sleepy eyes, and the Power to Rock the World …"

Whoa, Paula, that's a lot of stuff to sift through.

So, let's quiet our minds. Quiet times bring clarity.

"It is in our idleness, in our dreams, that the submerged truth comes to the top." —Virginia Woolf

Stop, silence your soul, and ask yourself if this rings true: that you're not just a hiccup in eternity, but eternity itself.

If this is true—which ancient scholars and masters, as well as their contemporary counterparts, espouse (and which science now realizes is true, if only with anecdotal evidence)—how does this make you view your own life? Does it help you realize that you do have a passion and a purpose, that you can choose to be brave and follow this dream? To stay authentic, to keep the faith, and to "choose greatly."

Joseph Campbell, a mid-twentieth-century professor, philosopher, and treasure hunter, memorialized this journey of being in paradise (or the shire or safe place) and hearing the call of adventure.

The "treasure" Campbell researched was a common thread of philosophy that connected all of humanity. He wanted to find a common link among all cultures throughout geography and history. He looked at all the ancient traditions and stories passed down by shamans throughout the millennia. He dissected each tradition, studied its myths, and found a basic pattern all cultural legends followed. He called the common structure of these stories a "monomyth" or hero's journey.

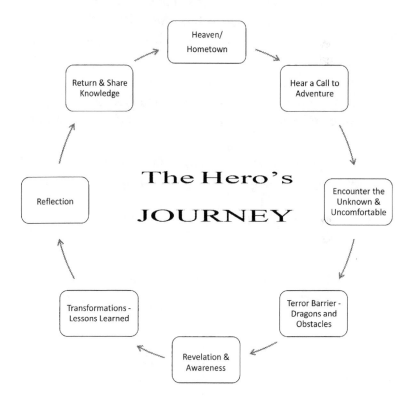

We start out in our comfort zone: our hometown or heaven. We feel something stirring in us, we hear a calling, or we see a need that must be filled or a wound that must be healed. We start the journey by leaving the safe place to fulfill this mission. We become afraid; we have never been this way before. We are outside our comfort zone. We want to quit because it's unknown and unnerving. But for some supreme reason, we keep going. We find helpers and mentors along the way. We know this path holds the answer even though we are fearful.

"The cave we fear to enter holds the treasure that we seek."

—Joseph Campbell

We encounter dragons, obstacles, and difficulties, but we have heard the call and recognize our purpose. We have a revelation. We realize that when we stay true to this reason, we are on our own path.

"When we follow our bliss, doors open where there were no doors before," Campbell wrote. "If you do follow your bliss, you put yourself on a track that has been there all the while, waiting for you."

We prevail. We are reborn and transformed. We march home valiantly to share this newly acquired knowledge we have gleaned, and we tell the tales of heroes.

And then we do it all again. We dream bigger (our beliefs grow, which allows bigger dreams). We fight mightier dragons, become braver, find a new path, and return home again.

You will have no idea where the path leads when you begin, but rest assured, it will lead you to your dreams. You will choose to go again.

All the stories you have ever been told and all the movies you have ever seen follow this same theme. *Star Wars, The Wizard of Oz, The Princess Bride,* and the Indiana Jones series are just a few. It is an eternal and inclusive journey that we recognize as noble. It is a path we all trod.

This is how we grow and expand as humans and, I submit, as spirits. We are either creating or disintegrating; there is nothing in between. It's a natural law, a scientific fact, a truth of the soul.

We need to keep jumping off that high dive, squealing in delight all the way down.

"The goal in life is to make your heartbeat match the beat of the Universe, to match your nature with Nature."

—Joseph Campbell

The universe expands, grows, changes, creates, and so must we.

There is an old axiom: "As above, so below." I propose that we as spiritual beings (as above) are on this journey of bravery. Living in a paradise, a safe spot, we choose to go on this journey to find the "thing that is supreme." So we return to earth, find our path, follow our dreams, slay our dragons, feel the ecstasy and the pain of our human life, and return home to rest and reflect. Then we begin it all again.

We as individual humans are also on a hero's journey (so below). We leave a safe place, journey to new lands, slay our own dragons, and then return home to rest and teach others. It continues to spiral up. When you access more awareness, more experiences, more beliefs and faith in the universe, you continue the hero's journey.

It all fits together so perfectly. As above (we willingly choose to journey here), so below (we willingly choose, upon awareness, to go after our dream and follow our bliss). This gives hope to the hopeless, as there is so much more than our five senses can perceive in this lifetime. There is a divine purpose, and we can use our six intellectual WIMPIR facilities to access that path.

You chose this existence, knowing there would be hard times.

You willingly chose to forget your divinity to experience earth to its fullest.

It's not forever; it's just for now.

You came for an adventure, so live it and follow your dreams.

You are a brave and noble spirit; you can never die.

"The privilege of a lifetime is being who you are."

—Joseph Campbell

Grab this life with both hands, appreciate it, love it, experience every single thing you can, live it to its fullest, follow your dreams, find your bliss, be brave, be strong, and be tenacious, but for heaven's sake *be!*

"Be, don't try to become." —Osho

"Before you can do something, you must first be something."

—Johann Wolfgang von Goethe

"The universe contains three things that cannot be destroyed: Being, Awareness, and Love." —Deepak Chopra

How Can We "Be"?

From my journal:

"Strawberries and cream, hot steaming coffee, sunny brisk day. Beginning of a new week … I make a mental note of chores.

"But right now, I'm in nature, warming in the sun, healthy, peaceful, content, loved, and loving. My body moves when I wish, my pantry is full, and the flowers are vibrant in this cool weather. Bills will be paid. My trees are swaying in the breeze. (They are my trees, you know. We have a relationship; they agree to stand tall and be strong and majestic, and I agree to admire them and stand in awe of their persistence and perfection.)

"The air is so clean; the sky is so blue. The leaves flutter to the ground in their final dance of the season.

"I scrape the last bit of cream from my bowl, admiring the slower-moving consistency of the liquid.

"The cream knows to be thicker. The trees know how to stand

as sentinels, stoic yet flexible. The leaves know how to fall, the sun how to shine.

"And I am learning to trust, to surrender, to be still in order to hear the silence. I used to think surrender was a bad word, weak and nonvictorious. I now realize when you softly surrender to the present, you find that is all you need. Those moments of more be-coming, more be-lieving, and more be-ing aware allow me to just be—embrace who I am at the moment with gratitude, realizing I am enough just the way I am. I don't have to struggle to be me. I just have to be present."

See yourself as a perfect spiritual being without limitation. When you do, you will find life easy.

"You will just follow your feet home." —From *A Knight's Tale*

"We are all just walking each other home." —Ram Dass

Exercise

Quiet your mind. Ask yourself the twelve questions posed at the beginning of this chapter. Really listen to the answers that come.

Chapter 10

- -

Write Your New Story

"Divorce the story, marry the dream." —Andy Dooley

"We become the stories we tell ourselves."
                    —Michael Cunningham

We think we have a historical story of our life. It is a chronological time line. It is over; it is reality. Nothing we can do about it now.

"It is our lot in life. It's not a lot, but it's our life."
                    (*A Bug's Life*)

But what if, just follow me here, we decide to do these things:

1. Marry our new dream (chapter 2)
2. Choose new beliefs that serve us (chapter 3)
3. Internalize new conditioning into our subconscious mind (chapter 4)
4. Quiet our minds (chapter 7)
5. Think, feel, and respond differently (chapter 5)
6. Recognize new serendipities in the now (chapter 6)
7. Take action (chapter 8)
8. Recognize and trust our true be-ing (chapter 9)

What if we realize we can use these newfound tools and go backward in our life?

Whaaat?

Yes, I said backward. We now have a completely different view of our current life. We have climbed the mountain a little higher and have a new, clearer perspective.

What if we take these ideas and the new perspective of our divinity on a stroll down memory lane?

In some instances, our childhoods were horrific, including perhaps physical, emotional, and even sexual abuse. We were victims of others, we have terrible scars, and we built strong shells around us to keep ourselves safe.

What if we use these new concepts to realize (use your imagination here and just pretend you believe it) that we are brave, daring spirits who choose to come here, knowing the hazards of time and space?

What if we view ourselves as heroes who, "choosing greatly," volunteered for another adventure, knowing the beginning might be a little rocky? What if we view ourselves as so courageous that we soldiered through it, and we now know we were never alone, always walking with our Higher Self? What if we realize those terrible things that happened were the dots along the way to get us to where we are now? That you wouldn't be the wonderful, compassionate person you are if these events hadn't occurred?

What if we realize all living things have shells (seeds, eggs, egos) that protect us until it's time to grow? When the seed meets the right environment, it cracks its shell and grows from inside with the amazing blueprint (the thing that is supreme) already and always inside. It be-comes the most amazing creation the world has ever seen and what we always were intended to be.

What if we view our past and retell it through the eyes of the new beliefs we have established? That we are brave souls who battled dangerous dragons and survived? That we were competent at creating our shells so we could survive until the time was right (the present moment) to emerge as an oak tree, a butterfly, or a Me?

"Just when the caterpillar thought the world was over, it became a butterfly." —Unknown

What if we learned to view with gratitude everything that has happened to us that led us here—to this space, this time, this knowledge?

Wouldn't that be wonderful?

This knowledge that the events in our past were necessary to bring us to this present moment was such an epiphany to me, I wrote a blog about it:

Epiphany: A Moment of Sudden Revelation or Insight

When I think of attempting to write about a specific epiphany in my life, I am, quite frankly, at a loss. I equate an epiphany with a bolt of lightning bringing sudden insight, or an out-of-body or near-death experience. I picture a large, flashing light bulb appearing over my head with an arrow pointing toward the word *truth*.

I would be disingenuous to write a story about this subject as I have never experienced such a revelation. I would also venture a guess that this would apply to the majority of people.

But what I can do is share some ideas with which, I believe, others can identify. Instead of the "light bulb" moments, I have what I call the "little twinkle light" moments—small coincidences that when they occur seem somewhat magical and demand my attention, if only for an instant. They cause me to catch my breath and wonder about the serendipity of life. Then, for a brief moment, I feel a connectedness to something larger than me.

Some examples that come to mind include a chance encounter with an old friend you were just thinking about, a book loaned to you that has the answer you were looking for, finding your keys in the same place you have looked for them three times, hearing a song on the radio that soothes your broken heart, taking a wrong turn and meeting the love of your life, or what you thought was a disaster turns out to bring something wonderful.

My life, in retrospect, has so many twinkle lights I could be mistaken for a Christmas tree. I was stood up by a blind date, but through a series of misadventures ended up meeting my husband. I received an email out of the blue that led me to my new profession. A post on Facebook allowed me to take my business to a much higher level. A beautiful, lamented bookmark appeared in a gutter as I was at a low ebb in my life with the quote "God blessed the world with special women like you." Rejections turned into much better opportunities. Chance encounters have led to cherished and unexpected friendships. They were all small detours and messages at the time, but together they have made all the difference.

These incidences alter your course, only minutely perhaps, and then you continue on your way. But if you take a closer look, with some time and distance between you and these occurrences, you see that these little glimmers of coincidence are actually all strung together like strings of twinkle lights guiding your path.

Your perception shifts. You see how the dots in your life begin to connect, all linked together by those strings of twinkle lights. You understand that the things that happened in your past, both good and bad, were required to get you to your current destination. You begin to see how everything that happened was a blessing. Your fear begins to melt into faith, and you have renewed appreciation that everything you've experienced has turned out for your benefit. You can see the magic and the infinite in the small serendipities of life.

You start telling a different story about how you lead a charmed and mystical life. What you previously perceived as failures have now turned into tales of bravery—how you overcome obstacles and stay the course, how you slay dragons and return home triumphant. You claim your rightful place in the cosmos and constantly become aware of, and appreciate, all the small twinkling messages from the universe.

These moments now come faster and more often, bringing bigger grins and better choices. Soon the twinkle lights are lighting each step you take.

You fear nothing because you now have faith in everything. You are in constant motion, growth, and love. Your world, your options, your ideas, and your dreams are in continuous expansion. Your path, although still only visible one step at a time, is guaranteed to lead you home.

And it all started with one twinkle light, showing you a glimpse of the infinite.

Hey, maybe this is an epiphany!

What if we were brave warriors who overcame difficult obstacles and prevailed? Write your story from this perspective. Write your past, knowing what you know now. Write it in detail, outlining your triumphs. Just write it. (I would love to read that story.) It will literally change your life.

Right now. Write now. Write your new story of your valiant life.

Here is how I rewrote my story:

I am, or was, a control freak. And I was very good at it. I know it caused me stress and anxiety, but I couldn't seem to help myself from bossing around the world.

Then one summer, I was fortunate enough to be coached by a dear friend, Michelle Jeffrey, using Debbie Ford's program, "The Dark Side of the Light Chasers." It is very insightful, and I highly recommend it.

At one of the coaching sessions, I was to identify a childhood event that stood out more than the others and describe it.

"When I was about twelve, my father, who owned a car

dealership in our small town, lost his business. He went from a respected business owner, president of Rotary, and deacon in the church to being unemployed and pretty much penniless. He had a nervous breakdown and stayed in his darkened bedroom for what seemed like months. He was broken.

"My stay-at-home mother went back to work as a secretary. I remember being sad by these events, but not broken. Months into this scenario, my father obtained a second-shift job at a factory thirty miles away, a humbling reality.

"Soon after things started to become somewhat normal, my family walked into a restaurant and my mother fell flat on her face. She didn't seem to trip. She didn't try to catch herself. After weeks of tests, and with her condition weakening, she was diagnosed with multiple sclerosis. She couldn't walk at all and spent months in the hospital. Now I was broken.

"My memory of this time has always been that I took control. I raised my younger sister, washed the clothes, cooked, cleaned, and became the parent to everyone. I had been vulnerable, and it scared the bejeebers out of me. I perceived the only path available was to be the one who did everything because I couldn't rely on anyone else to do it.

"I lived my life through those lenses, that paradigm. I controlled everything within my view. I soldiered on and became the boss of everyone—willing or not, it made no difference.

"I put myself through college and then law school. I started my own firm in 1981 when no other woman in town had ever done so. I projected my will onto anyone within range.

"I was self-sufficient and strong. I could do anything I put my mind to through sheer willpower. I never trusted anyone else to do anything for me. I was never going to feel vulnerable again.

"It served me well, to some degree. Until my heart "attacked" me and said, 'Just stop it. We didn't come here to be constantly tense, constantly strong, constantly in charge …Just stop it'. And when the anxiety attacks started, it was my body that said, 'We've got to get away from this crazy woman' and tried to run away from me. It got my attention.

"It started this journey."

Back to my friend and coach, who said, "Okay, now retell the story from a different perspective."

"Michelle, I just told you ..." But I repeated it, almost verbatim.

After the second time, she again said, "Can you tell it from a different perspective?"

Well, no, because this is how it went down, and once again I repeated the tale. Michelle had me repeat this eleven times, over three hours. Finally, she said, "How did you get the food to cook?"

Oh yeah, my dad went to the store.

"And the money to buy the food?"

My dad earned it.

"When did you have time to cook all those meals? Where did you obtain all that knowledge?"

Oh, okay, now that you mention it, each neighbor would take a day of the week and we would go there for lunch. Oh, and my parents' friends would bring casseroles almost on a nightly basis.

"Did you clean the entire house all by yourself every week?"

Hmmm, well, you know, my mother's girlfriends would come down sporadically and clean.

Memories flooded back. My grandparents were always available, my friends' parents volunteered to help and to take us places—all the people who helped started to become visible again.

Michelle asked one more time, "What is your perspective now?"

"The Universe had my back," I whispered.

This has made all the difference in my life. As a vulnerable child, I erected a story (a shell) to say I had done it all so I would never feel vulnerable again.

But from my new vantage point, my higher place on my mountain, I saw how all the dots connected, how the Universe had my back.

I met people I needed to meet, I obtained jobs that were

perfect for my needs, and I went to the schools I was supposed to go to. Small miracles happened at exactly the right instant. I coincidentally met the right men at the right time and had blessed relationships.

I was blessed with my darling daughter, Skylar, in my first marriage.

After my second marriage, we wanted another little one. I had three miscarriages and a failed in vitro procedure. I was devastated; I saw no rhythm or reason.

But then, oh but then, once again a miracle happened. Through coincidences too involved to explain, a friend stumbled on to a young, unmarried girl who wanted a family to love her unborn child and she did not believe in abortion. She had the baby and believed in us. The rest is an ongoing blessing.

If I hadn't had the prior disappointments, I wouldn't have our precious son, Connor. He still would have existed, but he wouldn't be with us. We needed each other more than words can say.

The Universe always has my back.

I would like to share another quick memory. My dad, in his earlier days, when he was president of the local Rotary, also became the president of the Little United Nations for the state of Kansas, an organization that brought programs to the area.

His proudest moment was in 1960 when he booked Eleanor Roosevelt to speak in Wichita, about thirty miles away. I was seven. My father had booked accommodations in the best hotel in Wichita for Mrs. Roosevelt and her entourage. The day she arrived, the hotel announced Mrs. Roosevelt was most welcome, but the "colored" members of her group would have to stay elsewhere. Mrs. Roosevelt refused to stay.

She asked my father to find other accommodations. He tried all the other hotels in Wichita he could think of. No one else would welcome them all.

Desperate, he called a friend in Wellington who owned a small, roadside motel—the type that was one long building with small rooms side by side and parking directly in front of the rooms. They welcomed the group with open arms.

The next morning, before they left for Wichita, my dad took my two sisters and me to meet her. We wore our Sunday best and curtsied constantly. We didn't really know who she was; she just looked like a kind, elderly aunt in a wheelchair.

(That's me, standing over Mrs. Roosevelt's right shoulder, behind my little sister.)

She greeted us with handshakes and hugs, complimenting us on our curtsies (a word you don't hear much anymore). I only spent a few moments with her, but my Higher Self whispered, "Remember this."

And now, her quiet spirit reaches out to me from the frumpy motel room and says, "Tell everybody to quit messing around! (I wanted to use another active verb that starts with "F," but she wouldn't let me.) It's time to change yourselves. It's time to change the world!"

In her own words, the following quotes are remarkable:

"It is better to light a candle than curse the darkness."

"You must do the things you think you cannot."

"The future belongs to those who believe in the beauty of their dream."

"You gain strength, courage, and confidence by every experience in which you really stop and look fear in the face."

"A stumbling block to the pessimist is a stepping stone to the optimist."

"Great minds discuss ideas, average minds discuss events, and small minds discuss people."

"Life must be lived and curiosity kept alive. One must never, for any reason, turn his back on life."

"You wouldn't worry so much about what others think of you if you realized how seldom they do."

"Do what you feel in your heart to be right, for you'll be criticized anyway."

"You can often change your circumstances by changing your attitude."

"Never mistake knowledge for wisdom. One helps you make a living; the other helps you make a life."

"Remember always that you not only have the right to be an individual, you have an obligation to be one."

—Eleanor Roosevelt

I now view meeting her as destiny, particularly as I see my history through new eyes.

Rewrite the story of your life, and make yourself the hero of the tale because you are. Look at your past with new eyes, a new perspective, and a new belief that things happened for a purpose and they will help you in the "now".

Comedian George Carlin once said, "The caterpillar did all the work, but the butterfly gets all the publicity." Now let's talk about that butterfly. Take your dreams and write, write, write.

Write out exactly how your life will look in one year, three years, etc., when your goal has been reached and your dream has come to fruition.

Write a complete story and feel the emotions you are going to experience when you live in that beautiful house by the ocean, run your nonprofit foundation, fly around the world, dance with your new love, or hold your new baby.

Write it in the present tense: "I am so happy and grateful now …"

Write it in as much detail as possible. Feel what you will feel when you acquire the goal—smell the pine trees, hear the ocean, or feel the soft baby—but engulf yourself in as much emotion as possible.

Use the phrases "I'm be-coming, I'm be-ginning, I'm be-lieving, and I'm be-ing." You can believe that things are rushing toward you, even if you haven't seen them yet. Start the process of believing things before you see them. It makes all the difference.

There is one caveat, however. Don't limit your dream to just one house, one ocean, or one career that you know of in the present moment. That limits the Universe. Use your imagination to set the goal, and let the Universe use its own imagination to fill in the blanks. Tell the Universe you trust him/her/it and that you know him/her/it has your back, and allow the Universe to fill your orders in the most magical way. While you're doing this, embrace the final emotion you want, but allow the Universe to direct your course.

Write it out and record it. Every one of those smartphones you can't seem to live without has a free recording app. Tell your story, present tense, with the amazing emotion you will feel when you arrive. Listen to it as many times as possible each day.

And you know what? That subconscious mind, not knowing the difference between real and imagined emotion, starts to vibrate differently because it hears you are happy. It begins to believe the story; it starts changing the paradigms and conditioning.

And as we learned before, the thermostat in your subconscious mind changes and begins showing you different bits of information. You respond differently to the stimuli. The Universe responds differently to you. Miracles begin to appear. Doors open that were once walls.

It can't help but happen. *It is the law.*

A great metaphoric story that describes the excitement and power you will feel is "The Golden Buddha":

Long ago in a small village there was a large, golden Buddha. The townspeople cherished this statue and took loving care of it. One day, word came that an invading army was approaching the village. The people didn't want their beloved statue to be pillaged, so they devised a plan to conceal it. They covered the entire statue with mud and sticks and dirt and concrete to hide the golden Buddha from the soldiers. As feared, the army occupied the town but miraculously ignored the statue because it was deemed worthless.

The army stayed for many years. All the people who knew about the covering of the golden Buddha died. Finally, the army withdrew.

Years later, a young monk was worshipping at the foot of the statue when a chunk of the concrete fell off, revealing a gleaming piece of the golden idol. He called the town and told them of his find. They all began peeling and chipping the protective cover from the figure, uncovering the golden Buddha.

This so parallels our own lives once we realize our power, our inheritance. We were all born golden; however, to "protect" us, our loved ones covered us with opinions and rules and false truths. This covering has been present our entire lives. We didn't even realize it was there. We forgot our brilliance.

Then one day, a piece of the covering falls off. You view things with a new perspective, you learn new information, you decide to go after your dreams, and you begin to see small miracles. You see the gold that was there all along. You want to continue peeling off the mud (the paradigms) and discover your golden destiny.

The study of alchemy purports to turn base metal into gold.

The study of the Law of Attraction turns *you* back into gold. When you study your true, amazing self, you can turn what you thought was an imperfect, boring life with a mortal shell into Divinity. You are made of stardust, powered by the Source that created the Universe.

You are on your way. You can't un-see, un-feel, or un-know what you have learned on this journey. You know there is more, you remember your heritage, and you reach for the thing that is *supreme*.

It is an exciting but perilous path. You have never been this way before. Everything looks foreign, different. It feels uncomfortable; you are afraid you will fail. You start questioning yourself.

"What if I fall?

"Oh, but darling, what if you fly?" —Erin Hanson

You will make up excuses regarding why you can't succeed—you are too young, you are too old, it is too late. You are not too young, you are not too old, and it is not too late. (Here's a fail-safe way to test if you are too old. Stop. Are you breathing? Then you're good.)

"The devil whispered in my ear, 'You're not strong enough to withstand the storm.' Today I whispered in the devil's ear, 'I am the storm.'" —Unknown

"Life isn't about finding yourself. Life is about creating yourself." —George Bernard Shaw

You have all the tools, knowledge, and bravery required to create that dream, and what you don't have right this minute, the Universe will provide when it is needed.

Here are a few words from Bob Proctor:

"It is time to understand more so we can fear less."

"There is no problem outside of you that is superior to the power within you."

"Be like a postage stamp. Stick to it until you get there."

Your closest family and friends will discourage you from going. They want you, for your own good, to stay where you are safe—the shire, the farmhouse in Kansas, the cupboard under the stairs. They don't want you to go; they are afraid they will lose you.

Here are some witty quotes you can drop into the conversation to help them understand:

"I can't start the next chapter if I keep reading the last one."

"I wasn't born to just pay bills and die."

"Life has no remote. I must get up and change it myself."

"My time as a caterpillar has expired. My wings are ready."

No matter what you encounter, remember this from Mike Dooley: "Whatever your problem or challenge may be, laugh at it, laugh long and hard. Because you are forever and it is temporary."

Okay, time to spread your wings and take that plunge. I'm right here if you need me, just an email away at: paula@ lawyerofattraction.com

And never, never, never forget: The Universe has your back.

"Ask, and it shall be given you; seek, and ye shall find; knock, and it shall be opened unto you." —Matthew 7:7

"It's impossible, said pride.
It's risky, said experience.
It's pointless, said reason.
Give it a try, whispered the heart." —Unknown

Exercise

Follow your bliss, find your dream, and live an amazing life.

Chapter 11

What Does Science Have to Do with It?

Caution: You are about to enter the Twilight Zone. Please be advised that the following information is mind-blowing and not for the faint of heart. Left-brain cynics will love it because it validates the Natural Laws of the Universe by using science, more specifically, quantum physics. For the rest of us, although it is extremely interesting, it is complicated, and understanding it is not necessary to live a magical life.

Science is just a set of experiments that are continually being revised. Old paradigms are being replaced by new facts. New experiments offer proof of ancient truths.

In *The Field* (p. xix), author Lynne McTaggart writes, "We tell ourselves stories in order to live. Of all the stories, it is the science ones that most define us. Those stories create our perception of the universe and how it operates … Although we perceive science to be the ultimate truth, science is finally just a story told in installments."

For nearly 350 years, the basic laws of physics, discovered by Sir Isaac Newton, have dominated the scientific arena. These laws stated that we lived in a three-dimensional universe of time and space, and there were certain fixed laws of motion that could not be modified. The universe worked like a huge mechanical clock and could not be altered or affected by man or his consciousness. Man was separate and apart from it and from each other.

Everything in science (physics) had to be measured to be verified. Because spirituality or consciousness could not be seen or measured, it had no place in science.

Science dismissed religion as a cultural myth. Thus, science was perceived as a threat to the tenets of the world religions. The two "philosophies" were as different as day and night and became alienated from one another. A huge rift was formed, which has shaped our culture for the last three centuries.

Science dictated that everything must be based on validated experiments to be believed. Anything else was a fairy tale. This dictate has been programmed into us since birth.

Rational people must use "the scientific method" when accepting or rejecting new ideas. This paradigm colors how we view the world. Logic, as well as common sense, tells us anything not provable by science is not the truth and must be rejected. It limits the framework of our lives.

"Believe nothing, no matter where you read it or who has said it, not even if I have said it, unless it agrees with your own reason and common sense." —Buddha

Our reason and common sense are controlled by the scientific facts that we have accepted as true. However, as science is only a story told in installments, new scientific breakthroughs deliver new, measurable facts that allow us, using logic, to believe new concepts and ideas.

There is also a part of our psyche that has always yearned for and intuitively recognized that there is something more to our lives, our world, and our destinies than a tangible fact. This *something* lies outside the rational train of thought. This yearning was normally relegated to an hour each week in church, if we chose to go. And even when we attended, it left some of us with more questions than answers and perhaps a sense of emptiness.

How do we coalesce these two concepts that control portions of our lives when they seem so separate and disconnected? Until recently, one was based on logic and the other on faith—an oxymoron that Einstein described this way: "Science without religion is lame, and religion without science is blind." He realized this division between science and spirituality was untenable.

The discovery of quantum physics in 1909 changed everything. The famous double-slit experiment revealed a new set of measurable facts that we can logically use as a basis for new beliefs.

A beam of light particles was shone at a barrier with two slits. When the light hit this barrier and shone through the slits, it was expected to scatter over a known pattern. However, as the light was being observed, it did not react that way. In some experiments, the beam of light became particles; in others, it became a wave. The *act of observation* determined how the light behaved. The same energy was expressing itself in different forms. The outcome of the experiment was determined by observation, by *consciousness* viewing it.

The pioneers of quantum physics peered into the subatomic world and were astonished by what they saw:

1. Matter was not matter. Sometimes it was one thing, such as a wave, and sometimes it was something else, such as a particle. It was just a quivering pocket of energy.
2. Even stranger, it could be many possible things at the same time.
3. These subatomic particles had no meaning in isolation, only in relationship to everything else.
4. One could only understand the universe as a dynamic web of interconnectedness; everything was connected to everything at the subatomic level.

5. Once the particles had been in contact, they remained in contact throughout time and space.

6. At the subatomic level, time and space did not appear to exist.

7. Most importantly, *our involvement*, our conscious involvement, was crucial. These particles existed in all possible states *until they were disturbed by our observation* and measurement. When our *consciousness* was present, they would settle down into a measurable particle or wave.

For the first time, science accepted consciousness as an integral part of how the subatomic world behaved. Our consciousness was essential in the creation of this reality. The particles would not settle down and become anything until a conscious observer viewed them. Consciousness actually created the event.

Consciousness—some part of us outside of our physical body—was now able to be measured and thus accepted by science. We once again became part of the universe, connected to all. Ironically, we were the most important part of the universe. The observer changed what was seen and was necessary for the creation of the event.

Science and consciousness had been reconciled, at least on a subatomic level. And everything is made up of subatomic particles.

This information allows new beliefs to form (that our consciousness creates our reality) and thus allows new paradigms to be installed into our subconscious mind. Belief is such an integral part in what we create. Without belief, our desire is merely a wish or a hope. With belief, which transforms our programming and thus our subconscious mind, we can create anything we choose to focus on.

Once again, in another category, current scientific findings have connected ancient truths with measurable data. For thousands of years, spiritual masters have referred to a "sea of energy" that unites us all. The Hindu tradition refers to it as the

Akashic records. The Buddhist tradition calls it nirvana. Ancient natives of the Americas left us information about a great web that connects the universe.

In the past, science had tried to discover if this sea of energy exists by determining if it could be measured but unfortunately failed. However, in 1986, with more delicate and sophisticated equipment, an Air Force-sanctioned experiment determined the "field" in fact existed and could be measured. *(Experimental Detection of the Ether,* E. W. Silvertooth, *Nature,* vol. 322, August 14, 1986, 590.)

Although mainstream scientists may argue its importance, the field is accepted as a fact.

This is sometimes referred to as the zero point field. When you reduce space to an absolute zero temperature in a vacuum, there should be no heat, energy, or light. However, there remains a sea of energy of subatomic particles.

This field "permeates, penetrates, and fills the inner spaces" of everything, wrote Wallace Wattles in his book *The Science of Getting Rich* (1903, six years before the discovery of quantum physics).

1. The field is a container of all things, for everything exists within this field. (Everything in the universe exists in this field.)
2. The field is a bridge between us and the world around us. (Whatever happens within us—our thoughts, emotions, feelings, and actions—is conveyed from our body to the world in this field.)
3. The field mirrors in the world around us what we claim to be true within us. (It shows us what our paradigms allow us to see, such as those fifty bits of information.)

Another experiment at the University of Geneva, Switzerland, on July 25, 1997, again proved how the field connects us. It was called the twin photon experiment. (Atoms are composed of photons.)

The scientists isolated a single photon and then split it into two, so each proton would have identical properties. In a specialized device, they shot each particle through fiber-optic cables in opposite directions, fourteen miles in length. They began to influence ("tickle") one of the photons, and then view the other particle. When they disturbed one, the other one fourteen miles away had exactly the same experience at the same moment. They were not physically connected.

They called this phenomenon the entanglement theory, which states, "Once matter is joined physically, it remains linked energetically even when no longer linked physically, regardless of the location." Science now tells us that what was once connected, stays connected within this field.

When we extrapolate this concept to its highest degree, we must refer to the time of the Big Bang. (It has been hypothesized when you take all the empty space from between all the atoms in the universe and compress it into a solid ball of matter, it will be the size of a single green pea.) At the time of the Big Bang this pea-sized ball of matter, because of a primal release of energy, began to expand into what we now call our universe. All matter was once physically connected in this same small space. This became the physical matter in the entire universe, and because all matter was once linked, it is still "linked energetically even when no longer linked physically, regardless of the location." Everything is still connected. We all came from the same small "pea," as everything was once physically connected. We are all made from the same matter; we are all stardust. When one particle is disturbed, it disturbs the entire universe. We are all connected energetically.

"What you do unto the least of these, my brethren, you do unto me." —Jesus

In another experiment, using the principal of holographic theory, science found that every piece of a hologram is the same as the whole. (Take any holographic image and cut it into as many minute pieces as possible, and you will discover each piece is the exact same image as the whole.) When we make a change to any one piece in the holograph, that change is made in the whole. Many scientists believe the universe is a hologram, and if you make a change in one place, it will be mirrored in the entire universe.

Now, referring back to the experiment on entanglement with the twin photons, the question was how did the information get from point A (one photon) to point B (the second photon)? There was no time difference between disturbing one photon and the other being disturbed. The information didn't have to travel; it was changed in the hologram, in the field, on an energetic level instantaneously—no effort, no time, or no distance. Something that has no specific space or time boundaries is referred to as nonlocality.

The implications are immense. We were once all connected. We are always linked energetically. We all exist in the field. When one part of the whole is changed, the change is seen instantaneously throughout the whole. We are powerful, no longer separate and alone. When we change ourselves, we change the cosmos.

"Be the change you wish to see in the world."

—Mahatma Gandhi

To create change, we must make it happen ourselves by thinking in a different way. When we change ourselves on an energetic (vibrational) level, it is felt throughout the universe.

Science is now virtually exploding with data that shows the ancient truths, the natural laws of the universe, are indeed measurable.

In 1992, a paper published in the *Bulletin of the Russian Academy of Sciences: Physics* gives us additionally needed information. The experimenters extracted all the air out of a glass vessel, leaving a vacuum. The only things that remained in the bottle were little photons of light, the unified field. The scientists measured where the photons were located in the bottle and found they were distributed randomly, as expected. They then injected human DNA into the vessel to see if it had any effect on the photons. They measured the location of the photons again after the DNA was inserted.

The photons went from a completely random order to an order that began to resemble the geometry of DNA strands. The human DNA started interacting with the field, having a direct, measurable effect.

The photons of light were described as behaving surprisingly and counterintuitively. "We are forced to accept the possibility that some new field of energy is being excited by the DNA" (P. P. Gariaev and V. V. Poponin, "Vacuum DNA Phantom Effect in Vitro and Its Possible Rational Explanation," *Nanobiology*, 1995).

"Science confirms human DNA directly affects the stuff the world is made of by direct communication with the field."

—Gregg Braden

There is additional scientific evidence that takes the concept of our DNA affecting the field to a higher level.

Scientists took human DNA from an umbilical cord (stem cells) and placed it close to a living heart. The heart is hundreds of times magnetically stronger than the brain. The scientists could measure the bio magnetics of the heart when different emotions were felt. The purpose of the experiment was to measure the DNA when exposed to different emotions.

The human subject was instructed to feel negative emotions. The DNA coil would tighten into a little knot when this emotion was projected, which stopped the DNA from performing its job (immunity system, aging, etc.)

The subject then felt positive emotions, and the DNA was

again measured. This positive emotion relaxed the DNA and allowed it to express itself to its fullest capacity. In the presence of positive human emotion (love, gratitude, appreciation) from the heart, the DNA relaxed so much that it almost started to replicate in a new, vitalized, healed state.

This was the first time it could be documented that human emotion changed the shape of the DNA and its ability to perform its functions. "Human emotion produces effects which defy conventional laws of physics." (Structural Changes in Water and DNA Associated with New Physiologically Measurable States. Glen Rein, Ph.D and Rollin McCraty, Ph.D *Journal of Scientific Exploration*, vol. 8, no. 3, 1994, 438–439).

The scientists found the greater the attention, the greater the effect. The more we feel intense emotions, the more we change our DNA. Our DNA affects the unified field. Our emotions therefore affect the unified field, the sea of energy connecting all the universe.

We are all entangled because we began as a solid mass before the primordial energy release (Big Bang theory). Our consciousness creates what is being observed (quantum physics double-split experiment). Anything once connected is always linked (twin-photon experiment). When we change one portion of the field, it transforms the whole (holographic theory). Our emotions affect our DNA. Our DNA affects the field. Our emotions, the vibration of each thought, affect the field. We are all connected and all powerful.

Professor John Wheeler, a peer of Albert Einstein, stated, "We had an old idea that the universe was out there and man was safely protected from the universe. Now we learn that just being an observer from a distance must be crossed off the book. We are now a participant, and we will never be the same."

Ancient Hindu, Buddhist, Jewish, and Christian traditions have been telling us this magical story from the beginning of time: We are one; we are connected. What you do to the least of these you do to yourself. We have the divine heritage of creating our universe and our reality. Love one another. It changes the world.

Remember what the Buddha said: "Believe nothing unless it agrees with your common sense."

We now have the scientific tools that allow us to use our logic and common sense to embrace the mystical aspect of our soul. This new paradigm permits us to also embrace the scientific discoveries through the words of our ancient sages. Science and spirituality have finally both come home.

Exercise:

Read this chapter as many time as necessary. You will be tested! ☺

Appendix

The Natural Laws of the Universe

The Law of Vibration states that everything vibrates and nothing rests. Vibrations of the same frequency resonate with each other, so like attracts like energy. Everything is energy, including your thoughts. Consistently focusing on a particular thought or idea attracts its vibrational match.

How to apply it: Focus on what you want instead of what you don't want.

The Law of Relativity states that nothing is what it is until you relate it to something else. Point of view is determined by what the observer relates to. The nature, value, or quality of something can only be measured in relation to another object.

How to apply it: Practice relating your situation to something worse than yours, and you will feel good about where you are.

The Law of Cause and Effect states that for every action there is an equal and opposite reaction. Every cause has an effect, and every effect has a cause. Be a cause for what you desire, and you will get the effect. All thought is creative, so be careful what you wish for—you will get it.

How to apply it: Consistently think about and act on what you desire so you can be effective at getting it.

The Law of Polarity states that everything has an opposite: hot/cold, light/dark, up/down, good/bad. In the absence of that which you are not, that which you are is not. Polar opposites make existence possible. If what you are not didn't coexist with what you are, then what you are could not be. Therefore, do not condemn or criticize what you are not or what you don't want.

How to apply it: Look for the good in people and situations. What you focus on, you make bigger in your life.

The Law of Rhythm states that everything has a natural cycle. The tides come in and go out, night follows day, and life regenerates itself. We all have good times and bad times, but nothing stays the same. Change is constant. Knowing that "this too shall pass" is great wisdom about life's ebb and flow.

How to apply it: When you are on a downswing, know that things will get better. Think of the good times that are coming.

The Law of Gestation states that everything takes time to manifest. All things have a beginning and grow into form as more energy is added to them. Thoughts are like seeds planted in our fertile minds that bloom into our physical experience if we have nourished them.

How to apply it: Stay focused and know that your goals will become reality when the time is right.

The Law of Transmutation states that energy moves in and out of physical form. Your thoughts are creative energy. The more you focus your thinking on what you desire, the more you harness your creative power to move that energy into results for your life. The universe organizes itself according to your thoughts.

How to apply it: Put your energy and effort, your thoughts and actions into attracting what you desire, and you will surely attract the physical manifestation of that energy.

CONTINUE THE JOURNEY!!!!!

Go to
www.lawyerofattraction.com

And come with me on a
Seven Day Challenge!
It's fun, It's free and it's transformative!
Learn how to take the ideas in this book and
incorporate them into your life. It just takes a
few minutes each day.
Commit to seven days of conversation with me as I
share how small choices can make enormous
differences in your life!
And it's scientifically proven to work!

Are you ready to PLUG INTO YOUR POWER?

Sign up at
www.lawyerofattraction.com/the-challenge/

JOIN NOW!
IT'S MY FREE GIFT TO YOU!

About the Author

Paula Kidd Casey-the Lawyer of Attraction-, discovered after practicing law for over 38 years, that the success she had achieved was unfulfilling and suffocating. After being immobilized by anxiety attacks because of this stressful life, she realized there had to be a better way to live. Doing extensive research, Paula found the life-changing secrets of living a fulfilling, abundant life. She reveals the science behind these secrets and how The Natural Laws of the Universe, when accessed correctly, produce this abundant, authentic life. She is a sought-after speaker, teacher and consultant for everyone wanting to access the magic of genuine abundance. She resides in Wichita, Kansas with her family.

Printed in the United States
By Bookmasters